AMERICAN HERITAGE
ILLUSTRATED HISTORY
OF THE UNITED STATES

The Aircraft Carrier U.S.S. Intrepid *shows the flag in the Mediterranean Sea in the 1950's.*
U.S. NAVY

FRONT COVER: *John F. Kennedy rides through Berlin with Chancellor Conrad Adenauer and Mayor Willy Brandt in June, 1961.*
JOHN F. KENNEDY LIBRARY

FRONT ENDSHEET: *Peter Hurd's* La Guardia at Dusk *depicts the less-than-frenetic pace of air travel in the late 1940's.*
CHRISTIE'S

CONTENTS PAGE: *On November 1, 1952, the United States tests the most destructive weapon invented by man—the hydrogen bomb—on the South Pacific island of Enewetok.*
DEPARTMENT OF DEFENSE

BACK ENDSHEET: *In 1965, Martin Luther King led 25,000 marchers from Selma to Montgomery, Alabama. Ralph Bunche is on Dr. King's right; Mrs. King is on his left.*
UNITED PRESS INTERNATIONAL

BACK COVER: *First Lady Eleanor Roosevelt (top left) played an active role in her husband's administration; a campaign button (top right) bears the popular nickname of Dwight D. Eisenhower, elected President in 1952; atop a Korean hillside, in snow and freezing weather, American G.I.'s (bottom) prepare to open fire on Communist forces.*
DOUGLAS CHANDOR; SUNNY SIT; UPI

AMERICAN HERITAGE
ILLUSTRATED HISTORY
OF THE UNITED STATES

VOLUME 16

DECADES OF COLD WAR

BY ROBERT G. ATHEARN *and*

MEDIA PROJECTS INCORPORATED

Created in Association with the
Editors of AMERICAN HERITAGE

CHOICE PUBLISHING, INC.

New York

Library of Congress Catalog Card Number: 87-73399
ISBN 0-945260-16-4

This 1988 edition is published and distributed by Choice Publishing, Inc., 53 Watermill Lane, Great Neck, NY 11021 by arrangement with American Heritage, a division of Forbes, Inc.

Manufactured in the United States of America

CONTENTS OF THE COMPLETE SERIES

Editor's Note to the Revised Edition
Introduction by ALLAN NEVINS
Main text by ROBERT G. ATHEARN
and MEDIA PROJECTS INCORPORATED

EACH VOLUME CONTAINS AN ENCYCLOPEDIC SECTION; MASTER INDEX IN VOLUME 18

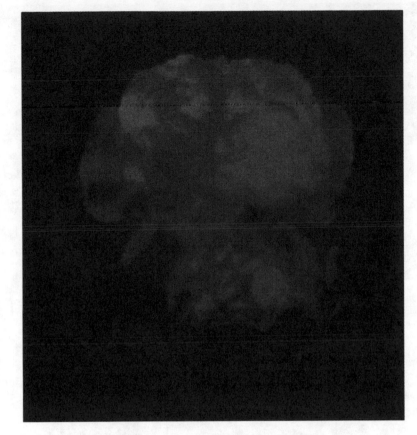

CONTENTS OF VOLUME 16

CHAPTER 46

Rebuilding a World in Ruins

The war was over. Armed forces that had at their peak numbered more than 12,300,000 were coming home— first in a trickle, then in a flood. The strongest, best-equipped fighting force in the history of the nation shrank to a military establishment of about 1,500,000 by 1947. The industrial might of the country spun on its axis to meet the pent-up domestic needs of a population that had lived for four long years with shortages and rationing. There were cars and trucks to be built and bought, highways, bridges, and tunnels to be constructed. There was housing to be erected, appliances and consumer goods to be manufactured and marketed. There were factories to be refurbished, priorities to be overhauled.

The nation faced the enormous task of converting from a wartime to a peacetime economy. Price and wage controls had to be lifted, but without touching off an inflationary spiral. Military advances in technology had to be diverted to domestic uses. American industry looked covetously to the enormous new pool of manpower that would quickly be at its disposal. Congress looked, too, and Congress worried, recalling the labor glut that had sent veterans of World War I into the streets selling apples in the 1920s. Nevertheless, there was a spirit of optimism abroad in the country. Resources in the United States were unparalleled. Personal and corporate savings were at an all-time high. They represented a pool of capital easily tapped to finance the conversion. Demand for goods and services was increasing, not only in America, where there was money to satisfy demand, but in war-torn Europe and Asia, where there was not. International credits needed to be established. Economies abroad would have to be rebuilt. Demand was an asset to the nation that could meet it, and America was not only the sole major industrial power fully intact at the close of the war, but also had made vast productive strides during it.

The devastation in Europe at the close of World War II is conveyed by a painting of Caen, Normandy, in 1944.

Conversely, unsatisfied demand was also a serious threat to the peace and security of the world. From this simple economic proposition emerged two basic goals that shaped and guided the foreign and domestic policies of the United States for the first 15 postwar years: (1) the need to prevent another worldwide conflagration and (2) the need to prevent an economic collapse. These were the goals of a mature and responsible world power, confident of its political and economic ability to satisfy the expectations of its own people. Indeed, these twin goals still inform much of the nation's policy. After World War II, the nation that had sought in 1920 to "return to normalcy" and a kind of economic status quo now endorsed the concept of a broadening middle class and a wider sharing of national wealth. The nation that had rejected the League for Nations in 1919 now embraced the need for a worldwide peacekeeping organization of all nations.

The nation's confidence was high. America had the resources, the technology, and the manpower. It had the means and the will to build and maintain a prosperous peace. Moreover, it had the most terrifying weapon in the world to enforce peace, the atomic bomb. Who would dare to threaten war? The United States and its Western allies soon got a startling answer.

Struggle in Europe

Joseph Stalin, dictator of the Soviet Union, saw the postwar scene in a different light. His nation was in partial ruin, yet stronger than it had ever been as the result of new defense plants erected during the conflict. The United States, driven by the need of an ally to engage Hitler's war machine from the east, had helped to "seed" Russia with the capital and tools to build a modern war potential of its own. In making the transition from war production to peacetime industrialization, Russia could not expect to compete in the international markets with the Americans, but it could isolate from the West a number of those markets in Europe and Asia. The Soviet Union set out to do so.

Eastern Europe was the first target of opportunity. It offered both markets and a manufacturing tradition—particularly East Germany, Czechoslovakia, Poland, and Hungary. As a result of wartime agreements with the Allies, Russia already occupied all of Eastern Europe. Maintaining their occupying armies there, the Russians proceeded by a combination of military presence and international political penetration to establish Communist regimes, with close ties to Soviet economic and military policy. The gateways of trade between Eastern and Western Europe slammed shut, prompting Winston Churchill, Britain's wartime Prime Minister, to comment in 1946: "An iron curtain has descended across the Continent." By 1948, the Communists had seized power in Albania, Bulgaria, Czechoslovakia, East Germany, Hungary, Poland, Rumania, and Yugoslavia. Powerful Communist parties, built around the nuclei of partisan underground fighters, were gaining in-

Among the Communist leaders celebrating Joseph Stalin's 70th birthday in 1950 were Mao Tse-tung, Nikita Khrushchev, and Vyacheslav Molotov.

fluence in France and in Italy; and Russia was gazing rapaciously toward Greece and strategic Turkey, the key to control of the eastern Mediterranean.

The Communists were also turning their attention to the many new nations gaining independence after World War II. These included Burma, India, Indonesia, Israel, Pakistan, and the Philippines, all of which became independent by the end of 1949. In all cases except the Philippines, which had been a U.S. possession, the former colonial rulers were weakened by the war and were no longer able to resist their colonies' demands for freedom. One by one—with bitter factional infighting in most cases— the new nations took their place on the stage of world affairs, with many more to follow, especially in Africa in the 1960s. Waiting in the wings in some former colonies were Soviet-oriented Communist cadres, ready to move in should the new governments prove to be weak or unstable. Thus, the stage was set for a worldwide confrontation between capitalist and communist systems.

If Stalin's territorial aims for Communism were to be contained, the United States would have to act quickly, particularly in the industrial nations of Europe that had been devastated by the war. But America, once in such a hurry to win the war, was now preoccupied with domestic problems. Demobilization became the first concern of the country. An elaborate "point system," which took into account length of service, length of time in a combat theater, military awards, and service-connected disabilities, ruled the mustering-out process. It was designed to avert the abrupt weakening of the armed forces, as well as to prevent returning servicemen from overpowering industry with job demands. The system was equitable; however, many believed it to be much too slow. At the urging of President Harry S. Truman, Congress enacted other measures to ease the demobilization. There was a one-year unemployment bonus of $20 per week available for each qualified ex-serviceman unable to find work. Hundreds of thousands took advantage of

1357

this bonus, partly as a respite from the activities of war, largely as a necessary compensation until they could find suitable jobs. Perhaps the most enlightened measure was the offer of free tuition and maintenance for returning servicemen who wanted to continue their education. Veterans by the millions returned to school. Intended primarily to blunt the effect of demobilization, this single government program became the root of vast sociological change and great economic advances. In the decade between 1940 and 1950, before the impact of postwar population growth was felt in the classroom, school enrollment rose by more than 1,500,000. It had risen by less than 100,000 in the preceding decade. The example of mature young men delaying the beginning of their work careers and struggling, often with young families, to better themselves touched off an education boom. This, in turn, was to provide the industrial, commercial, and professional sectors of the nation with a higher degree of literacy and competence than ever before. As a result, 20 years after the war, the educational level of the average American had risen a full three years. The average American adult in 1945 had a grade-school education with one year of high school. By 1965, the typical American was a high school graduate, and the illiteracy rate was down to 2.4% of the adult population.

The price of peace

In the immediate postwar years, however, gaps in educational and economic opportunities available to Americans became visible. President Truman sought to press civil-rights legislation; however, together with attempts to deal with many of the other dislocations of the conversion from war to peace, the effort was to carry a high political price. Shortages among various goods and commodities continued through 1946. Truman fought for continuing price controls in certain important areas of the economy. However, the mood of the country argued against him. America had had enough of regulation, and as price controls vanished, consumer prices began to rise. Organized labor reacted with demands for higher wages, and the result was a series of crippling strikes beginning in late 1945 that one time or another over the next two years closed down much or all of the nation's automobile, coal, railroad, airline, steel, shipping, and meat-packing industries.

The public wrath was directed at Truman. He was blamed for the grinding pace of demobilization, for the shortages in consumer goods, and for the various dislocations that inevitably occur when a nation leaves the warpath and turns to peace. To the Democratic party went the blame for the seemingly unlimited power of labor to strike crippling blows at the important areas of the nation's economy. Many felt that the culprit legislation was the 1935 National Labor Relations Act (Wagner Act), which strongly backed the right of labor to organize and bargain collectively. The Republicans skillfully exploited the argument that this law gave labor too much power. "Had enough?" demanded the G.O.P. publicists. The pendulum of American political opinion appeared to be swinging back to the right, after 14 years of social reform.

The Congressional elections of 1946 tended to confirm this. They were a Democratic disaster. After enjoying comfortable majorities in both houses of the 79th Congress, the Democrats tumbled ingloriously to minority roles in each. They lost nine seats in the Senate, giving the Republicans a 51 to 45 majority; and they lost an unprecedented 54 seats in the House, providing a 245 to 189 Republican majority there.

Publicly undismayed, Truman continued to press for modest civil-rights legislation, and he took up the fight against what many labor leaders felt to be retaliatory labor legislation. He lost on both issues. Few new social-reform measures were enacted, and a new labor law—the Taft-Hartley Act of 1947—was passed over Truman's veto. This measure outlawed the "closed shop" that had prevented a union plant from hiring nonunion personnel. It restricted the union shop, which had obligated workers to join the resident union within a set period of time. The new law also enabled the government to delay a strike for an 80-day "cooling off" period if the national interest was threatened.

Balked in his domestic program by a strong conservative coalition in Con-

French farmers learn to use up-to-date American-built tractors sent to them as part of the 1947 Marshall Plan to help revitalize the economy of Europe.

Children stand on what remains of a bombed building in Berlin in 1948 to watch an American plane delivering its cargo of coal in the Berlin airlift.

gress, Truman still managed to carry on a vigorous and farsighted foreign policy. Alert now to the dangers of a power vacuum in Europe, the United States proclaimed in March, 1947, a policy of military and economic aid to nations threatened by Soviet ambitions. "I believe that it must be the policy of the United States to support free peoples who are resisting attempted subjugation by armed minorities or by outside pressures," President Truman said in his statement to Congress. Later called the Truman Doctrine, this policy was basically designed to contain communism. As a start, $400,000,000 in aid was allocated to Greece and Turkey. Three

months later, in June at Harvard University, Secretary of State George C. Marshall proposed a vast program of aid for the free nations of Europe (the European Recovery Program) to help rebuild their shattered economies. The Marshall Plan, the first in the history of the world to offer economic assistance to friends and former foes alike, was to become the first and the most successful of American foreign-aid programs. Funded by more than $12,000,000,000 in American economic aid, industry, agriculture, and mineral production in Western Europe revived, and the free nations began to draw new breath on their own.

Russia's reaction to these initiatives

The Wall—grim symbol of the Cold War—was built in 1961 to prevent East Germans from escaping to freedom in West Berlin. It is 29 miles long and 8 to 12 feet high. Here it seals off the Brandenburg Gate from the British sector. The barbed wire is put up to keep West Berliners from straying into a no-man's land.

was to abrogate the four-power agreement of free access to Berlin. In June, 1948, the Soviets blockaded the land and water routes into Germany's old capital city, 110 miles inside the Russian zone. No amount of diplomatic persuasion or world opinion could remove the roadblocks. The aim was to force the Western powers to give up their occupation zones in Berlin. The West responded with one of the strangest supply operations in history. Throwing together a collection of C-47 and C-54 cargo planes, the United States airlifted potatoes, coal, meat, vegetables, and all of the other staples of a modern city into Berlin's Tempelhof Airport. For 24 hours a day, seven days a week, for more than ten months, the supplies poured into the blockaded city. The Russians, beaten at their gambit, finally removed the roadblocks in May, 1949. But by that time, the nations on both sides of the North Atlantic rim had pooled their armed forces in a joint command under the new North Atlantic Treaty Organization (NATO) to provide a military presence to counter the Russian divisions in Eastern Europe.

Meanwhile, in Japan the United States faced a different, and no less demanding challenge. After General Douglas MacArthur received the Japanese surrender aboard the U.S.S. *Missouri*, he rode into Tokyo as Supreme Allied Commander for the Allied powers. The scene along the General's route was as blasted as a moonscape. As far as the eye could see, only a few surviving buildings poked up from the heaps of rubble. Except for MacArthur's motorcade, there were no other automobiles in evidence. MacArthur's entry was watched in silence by scarecrows of men and women who seemed too dazed to understand what was happening. For the next five years, MacArthur ruled Japan with all the powers of a military dictator. To the surprise of many, he was neither vengeful nor insensitive to the people of the defeated and humiliated nation.

Japan was stunned from the horror of the world's first atomic bomb attacks. Tokyo, Yokohama, and other major cities had been devastated by B-29 fire-bomb raids. In the four years of war with the United States, more than 1,270,000 Japanese had been killed in action. The heavy bombings of the Japanese mainland toward the end of the war had claimed the lives of 670,000 civilians.

Food and clothing were scarce and the Japanese people were desperate. MacArthur immediately set up Army food kitchens. When supplies were slow in coming, he cabled Washington: "Give me bread or give me bullets." Turning his attention to political reform, MacArthur was determined to make Japan more democratic and to prevent militaristic elements from ever dominating the government again. The centerpiece of MacArthur's achievement was a new constitution. It reorganized the government, abolished the feudal aristocracy, guaranteed the basic liberties of the people, granted equality to women, and enabled labor unions to bargain collectively. Most remarkable of all, the new constitution renounced war as an instru-

It was Truman's hard campaigning, much of it at whistle stops like this one in Idaho (above), that gave him his victory in 1948. The day after election, he gleefully displayed the Chicago Tribune's *premature headline (below).*

ment of national policy. Japanese land, sea, and air forces were dissolved, except for a small national security group.

An upset victory

Truman's hands-off policy toward MacArthur's rebuilding of Japan was an important factor in the success of the American occupation. But this was not apparent to the American electorate as the 1948 elections approached. Nor was Truman's remarkable performance in Europe fully understood. Moreover, many of the President's domestic programs had failed to get through Congress. A Republican victory seemed to be in the air. Truman's espousal of civil rights and his fight against the Taft-Hartley Act had lost him the support of the conservative Southern leadership. On the other hand, his failure to move Congress with a middle-of-the-road approach cost him the support of the progressive wing of his party. As November approached, the Southerners formed a states' rights (or "Dixiecrat") faction and bolted the Democratic convention to nominate Strom Thurmond, Governor of South Carolina, for President. The liberal wing formed the Progressive party and nominated former Vice-President Henry A. Wallace.

The Republicans confidently selected New York Governor Thomas E. Dewey, and the party and its candidate settled back to await the inevitable victory. As the campaign began, Dewey avoided specific expressions on issues and ran as a statesman. In the opinion of the pundits, he was a certain winner. Cast in the role of the underdog, Harry Truman soon became the hardest fighting underdog to stride across the Presidential campaign scene in modern times. Denied for the most part the editorial support of the nation's press, he took his campaign to the grass roots and, crisscrossing the country, the President denounced the Republican 80th Congress as a "do-nothing Congress." He elaborated with specifics, charging the Republicans with the responsibility for everything that was wrong with life in these United States. "Give 'em hell, Harry!" was a frequent response from the large crowds drawn to his spirited campaign. Labor rallied to him, and he raced back and forth across the Midwestern wheat and corn belts in a special train, hardly missing a whistle-stop in a determined bid to unify the farm vote. In one of the most stunning upsets of American political history, Truman carried 28 states with 303 electoral votes, Dewey carried 16 states with 189, and the states' rights Dixiecrats, four Southern states with 39.

Now elected President in his own right, Truman sought to press his Fair Deal program of social-reform measures, but the Democratic 81st Congress, while seeking to modify some of the more stringent passages of the new Taft-Hartley Act, was little more responsive to the President's wishes than the Republican 80th. And soon the man from Missouri who entered the Presidency with few pretensions of greatness would once again find his role cast on a global scale.

The Museum of Modern Art, New York City.

THE REVOLUTION IN AMERICAN ART

In the early 1940s, as the United States entered World War II, the predominant painting styles in this country were regionalism and social realism (*see Volume 14*), both indigenous to America and neither much influenced by modernist European painting. But with the war came changes that had been fermenting for two decades, and by 1946 a new group of painters—some with origins in Europe, others with roots in the American heartland—had created the most powerful original movement in the history of American art: abstract expressionism. This term, which had earlier been used to describe the work of Wassily Kandinsky, was now applied to the highly individualistic paintings of Jackson Pollock, Barnett Newman, Willem de Kooning, Clyfford Still, Franz Kline, Mark Rothko, and others. They received official recognition in the 1951 landmark show Abstract Painting and Sculpture in America at New York's Museum of Modern Art. Although sometimes referred to collectively as The New York School, these artists cannot be narrowly categorized; each was experimental, personal, and—generally—not representational. The diverse genius of this group made New York at mid-century the avant-garde capital of the world, even displacing Paris.

By the mid-1960s, Pop (for "popular") Art had arrived. The first major reaction against abstract expressionism, its leaders included Robert Rauschenberg, Jasper Johns, Roy Lichtenstein, Jim Dine, and Andy Warhol. Like their predecessors, their work was diverse, but they had in common a fascination with the most blatant and pervasive everyday images in America: flags, commercial art, comic strips, clothing, and celebrities.

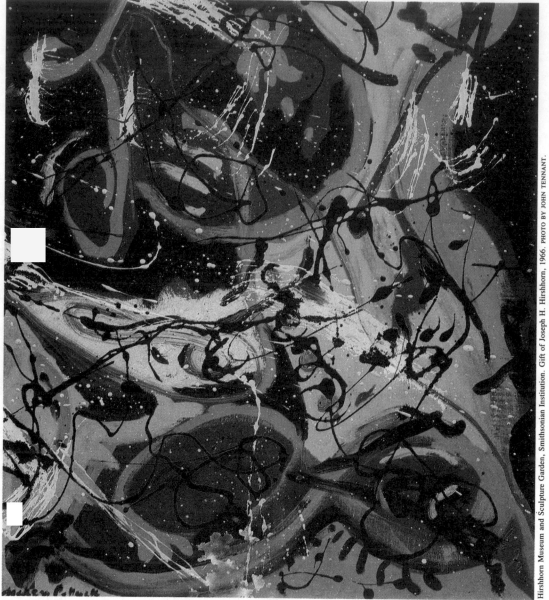

Composition with Pouring II. 1943. Jackson Pollock.

Blue, Orange, Red. 1961. Mark Rothko.

Woman (recto). 1948. Willem de Kooning.

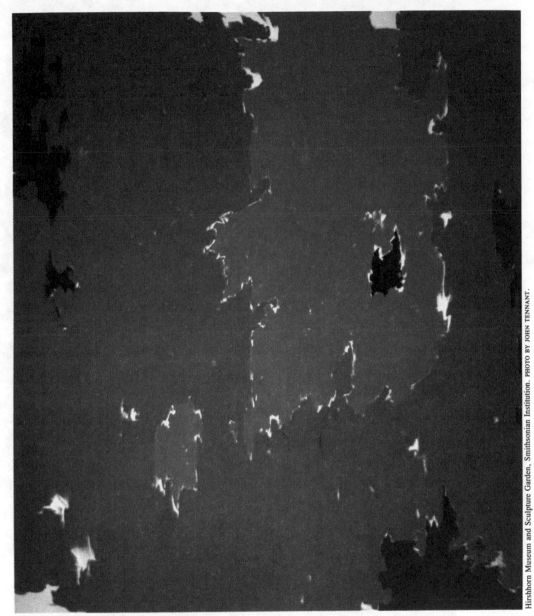

1950–A No. 2. 1950. Clyfford Still.

Covenant. 1949. Barnett Newman.

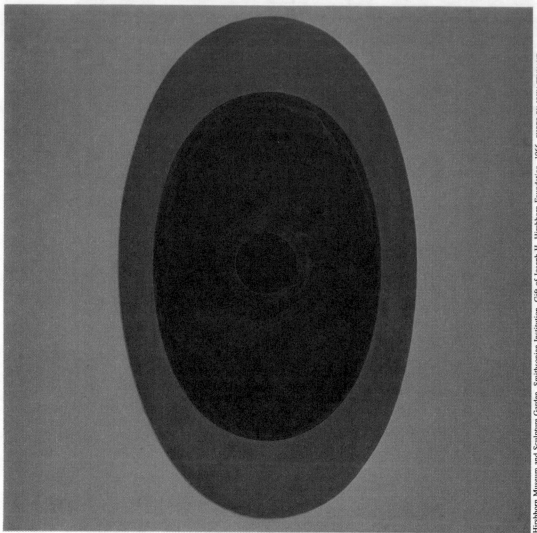

Almondite. 1963. Kenneth Noland.

Point of Tranquility. 1958. Morris Louis.

Untitled. 1957. Franz Kline.

Hirshhorn Museum and Sculpture Garden, Smithsonian Institution. Gift of Joseph H. Hirshhorn, 1966. PHOTO BY JOHN TENNANT.

Jersey. 1958. Ellsworth Kelly.

Flag. 1958. Jasper Johns.

Flesh Striped Tie. 1961. Jim Dine.

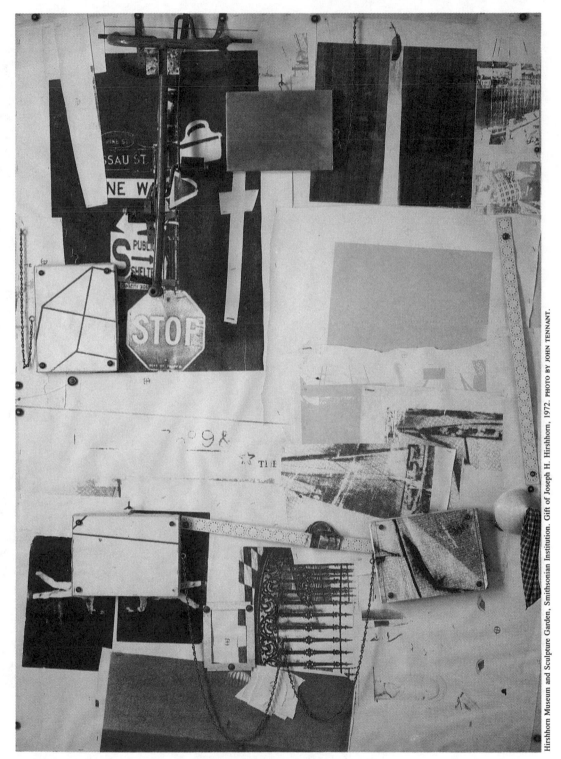

Fossil for Bob Morris, N.Y. 1965. Robert Rauschenberg.

1380

Modern Painting with Clef. 1967. Roy Lichtenstein.

Hirshhorn Museum and Sculpture Garden, Smithsonian Institution. Gift of Joseph H. Hirshhorn, 1972. PHOTO BY JOHN TENNANT.

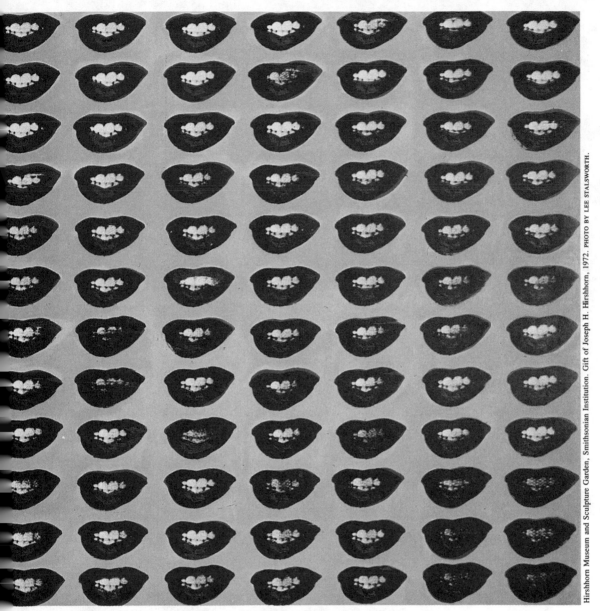

Marilyn Monroe's Lips. 1964. Andy Warhol.

THE COLD WAR HEATS UP

Although Communist expansion in Europe seemed to reach its high-water mark with the Berlin blockade, Communist power and prestige were by no means waning. The West was to receive three damaging blows in three years, each more shaking than its predecessor. In 1949, the Soviet Union exploded an atomic bomb. Up until this moment, Stalin's ambitions had always been tempered by his knowledge that he risked a shooting war in Europe at great peril to his homeland. But with atomic arms in Soviet hands, America's monopoly of the "ultimate weapon" was effectively checked, and the tentative peace of Europe could be threatened once again by the superior numbers under arms behind the Iron Curtain. It was a rude awakening for Americans accustomed to believing that the Soviet Union, while strong, was no technological match for the United States. It had become fashionable to believe that the Soviets, in

A U.S. Marine rocket battery launches a barrage against Communist forces during the Communist offensive in Korea in 1951.

one popular phrase, "could not produce a decent flush toilet." The Soviets had in little more than four years duplicated the world's highest technological achievement, the release of atomic energy. Of course, the U.S.S.R. had had the services of captured German scientists as well as the aid of skilled and highly organized espionage agents who had penetrated the atomic arsenal of the West. Public opinion might console itself with these thoughts inside the United States. To the rest of the world, however, a new superpower had arrived. To cope with the new threat, NATO was strengthened. Eventually, it would grow to 51 divisions, backed up with American-equipped air support and the U.S. Sixth Fleet prowling the Mediterranean.

The next blow fell in Asia. Communist revolutionaries had been fighting for control of China since long before World War II. With the emergence of Chiang Kai-shek's Nationalists from the ruins of Sun Yat-sen's Republic, the Communists under Mao Tse-tung retreated more than 1,000 miles into the remote interior, there to await their time. It came at the

Chinese workers march in the National Day Parade, October 1, 1950, commemorating the first anniversary of Mao Tse-tung's Communist regime.

close of World War II. With Japan defeated and withdrawn from the Asian mainland, Mao struck. In four years, he brought Chiang's Nationalists to decisive battle and drove them out of China, across the Formosan Strait to the island of Formosa, which they renamed Taiwan. With American aid, Chiang turned Taiwan into a military and industrial stronghold. Free China's presence was further maintained at the United Nations, where Chiang's government held the fifth seat on the U.N. Security Council.

But Communists controlled a more tangible Asian reality—one-sixth of the world's surface, one-fourth of the world's population. To the uncommitted nations, the nuclear feat and the territorial accomplishment were impressive performances. The last of the three blows was struck in Asia also.

War in Korea

Since 1910, Korea had been occupied by the Japanese, who had annexed the country from China following the Sino-

1386

Japanese War. This occupation ended with the Japanese surrender in 1945. However, in the closing days of World War II, Russian troops had moved into the northern part of Korea. Soviet domination of North Korea was recognized at the Potsdam Conference in July, 1945, and Korea was divided into two zones at the 38th parallel, with the Communists controlling North Korea and the United States occupying South Korea. Once the Republic of Korea was established in the south in 1948, the United States began to withdraw its occupation troops. In 1950, the U.S. military presence in South Korea dwindled to approximately 500 officers and men in a military advisory group assigned to help improve the poorly trained and ill-equipped Republic of Korea Army.

On June 25, 1950, North Korean soldiers stormed across the 38th parallel in a stunning surprise attack. They quickly drove the thinly deployed South Korean troops and their American advisers into a small corner of southeastern Korea around the port city of Pusan. The American response was immediate. U.S. air, ground, and naval forces in Japan and the Philippines were ordered to Korea by President Truman. The issue was brought before the United Nations Security Council. At the time, the Soviet Union was boycotting the Security Council because China was represented by the Taiwan government rather than that of mainland China. With the Soviet delegation absent, the Security Council adopted a U.S. resolution calling for armed intervention in the conflict. Fif-

teen other nations joined the United States in sending units to Korea. General Douglas MacArthur, still heading the occupation government in Japan, was placed in command of the U.N. forces.

MacArthur quickly realized that it would be difficult to break out of the Pusan perimeter without a long, costly period of trench warfare. So he mounted a brilliant amphibious invasion at Inchon on the west coast near the 38th parallel. Seoul, the South Korean capital, was recaptured in bitter fighting. Meanwhile, American and Korean forces in Pusan broke out of their perimeter and raced north to link up with the Inchon invasion troops moving east. To escape being trapped, the North Koreans fled back over the 38th parallel. The U.N. forces pursued them north to the Yalu River, the border between Korea and China.

The U.N. command spoke of having the troops home by Christmas, 1950, but the Communists were not finished. In late November, a huge force of 200,000 Communist Chinese soldiers poured across the Yalu River. In a series of massive infantry assaults, the Chinese forced the U.N. troops back across the 38th parallel. Seoul was recaptured by the Communists. It was not returned to South Korean control until the U.N. forces began pushing north again in the spring of 1951. The war then settled into a bloody seesaw, with the U.N. forces gradually moving north to establish a line in North Korea that could be defended while peace negotiations began.

In one of the most dramatic events of the war, Truman relieved MacArthur of his Korean command on April 11 and replaced him with General Matthew B. Ridgway. America's most popular warrior and the President had been clashing on the overall conduct of the war for months. MacArthur wanted to use all possible means to win it.

Documents in the dispute are still classified. MacArthur, however, is known to have advocated attacking Chinese territory, and it has been suggested that he wanted to use nuclear weapons. Truman wanted to avoid at all costs an open war with China, which would have involved committing American forces to the vast Asian mainland as a first step and would, as a second, have provoked,

perhaps beyond settlement, a nuclear confrontation with the Soviet Union. MacArthur submitted quietly to recall, allowing his many admirers in Congress and in the press to do his speaking for him. In an address to a joint session of Congress, he skirted the specifics of the dispute and in a moving peroration foretold his eclipse: "Old soldiers," he concluded in his husky baritone, "never die, they just fade away."

The old soldier carried the emotional day. However, the President had reinforced the principle of civilian authority over the military. The war dragged on, domestic problems multiplied, high-level scandals of influence peddling rocked

In snow and freezing weather, a machine gun—set into a Korean hill across from a Communist position—is about to be fired by American soldiers.

the Truman administration, and grave doubts arose concerning the internal security of the United States. Truman announced early in 1952 that he would not be a candidate for reelection, and the Democrats chose the liberal and highly accomplished Governor of Illinois, Adlai E. Stevenson, as their candidate. However, it was clearly "time for a change." Truman's election of 1948 was judged as more of a performance of political virtuosity than an expression of the mood of the country, which was still looking for a respite from conflict, both foreign and domestic. The Republicans were taking no chances. They nominated the immensely popular Dwight D. Eisenhower, World War II Supreme Commander of Allied forces in Europe, the postwar president of Columbia University, and, after December, 1950, Commander of the Supreme Headquarters of Allied Powers in Europe (SHAPE), NATO's armed forces. The Korean War and the global Communist threat occupied center stage in the 1952 Presidential campaign. Eisenhower trod gingerly around the thorny problem of conducting limited warfare in a nuclear age. He suggested that he would bring the conflict in Korea to an end after making on-site evaluations. "IKE WILL GO TO KOREA" said the headlines, and Americans, in their frustration with the war, were comforted by the thought of this sincere man applying his knowledge and experience as Commander-in-Chief. He won 442 electoral votes to the hapless Stevenson's 89. A Republican Congress accompanied him to power.

While fulfilling a campaign promise to make an inspection tour of Korea, Eisenhower eats with men from the front.

Eisenhower began his administration with high energy, convinced that he could bring order and responsiveness to the vast confusion of interests that had increased with the growth of the federal establishment over 20 years of Democratic administration. "Poor Ike," commented Harry Truman. "He'll say, 'Do this' and 'Do that' and nothing will happen." Truman was to prove largely correct. The collision of the high-powered army general and inertia-bound bureaucracy shot off an occasional spark, but it hardly altered the working pace or the size of big government. Too many interests contended for attention in the formulation and execution of the nation's federal policies.

Peace is achieved

Foremost of Eisenhower's problems was the Korean War. Armistice talks had actually begun in July, 1951, at Kaesong and had been moved that October to the small border village of Panmunjom. They dragged on with interruptions for two years. Eisenhower made his inspection tour of Korea with little effect other than a marked rise in morale. But finally, on July 26, 1953, armistice terms were agreed to, and the shooting ended 12 hours later. The Asian Communists were not to follow the Korean example of conventional battle-line warfare again. Two thousand miles south of Korea, the French, trying to hold on to their old colonial possessions in Indochina, were threatened by Ho Chi Minh. In the spring of 1954, Ho's forces drew the French into the valley stronghold of Dien Bien Phu in North Vietnam and on May 8 defeated the French decisively. Vietnam was partitioned along the 17th parallel, and thereafter the defense of the South and its government was to become increasingly an American responsibility. After Dien Bien Phu, the United States established with seven other nations the South East Asia Treaty Organization (SEATO). It was never to gain the strength of its Atlantic counterpart, NATO, and the multinational commitments to SEATO—aside from continuing American presence in Far Eastern military bases resulting from the 1948 Treaty of San Francisco with Japan—were no match to NATO.

The American public, after the close of the Korean War, paid little attention to these moves. They were more concerned with the growing controversy over internal security and civil liberties. Beginning in 1948, the United States was to pass through nearly seven years of domestic uproar over the amount of influence exercised by Communists or fellow travelers on U.S. policy. The denunciation of Alger Hiss, once a trusted adviser in the State Department, as an agent for the U.S.S.R., touched off the issue. Hiss denied specific charges leveled at him by former Communist Whittaker Chambers, but he was convicted two years later of perjury. The issue, originally raised in the House Un-American Activities Committee, was fanned to white heat in 1950 with the emergence of an obscure Midwestern Senator, Joseph R. McCarthy (Republican, Wisconsin), who claimed but never proved that he had a list of 205 Communists in the State Department. Having gained prominence with his charge, McCarthy next gained power to exploit it when the Republican 83rd Congress took office in 1953. As the ranking Republican on the Senate Committee on Government Operations, he became its Chairman. He also took over the chairmanship of its subcommittee on investigations, and from this position he launched a series of hearings and investigations that had the effect of suggesting that the government was riddled from top to bottom with Communists and their sympathizers. To mounting demands

The end of the investigations by Joseph McCarthy (left) came in 1954 when many Senators, like Ralph Flanders (right), began to criticize his methods.

that he be required to prove, not merely state, his charges, the country split into pro-McCarthy and anti-McCarthy camps. The issue grew venomous when McCarthy's camp began equating anti-McCarthyism with pro-Communism. McCarthy himself burst this overinflated bubble. In 1953, he attacked General George C. Marshall, former Secretary of State, as a Communist agent. Eisenhower, aloof but concerned as the controversy grew less reasonable, defended his former chief. McCarthy's reaction—

incredible as it might seem—was to suggest that Eisenhower himself was somehow in league with the Communists. As the Wisconsin Senator's credibility waned, the Senate convened a special committee to investigate charges brought by the army as the result of the Senator's inquiry into subversive activities. Following the so-called Army-McCarthy hearings, which were televised nationally, the Senate, on December 2, 1954, voted 67 to 22 to condemn McCarthy for abuse of the Senate and

1391

This giant statue of Joseph Stalin was toppled by students and workers in Budapest on October 23, 1956, the day that the Hungarian revolt began.

insults to its members. McCarthy's power and the fear his methods had stitched into the politics of the early 1950s were over.

Meanwhile, the uneasy peace of Europe survived a series of crises. The sinister hegemony of Joseph Stalin over the Communist world had ended with his death in March, 1953. New initiatives were taken between East and West. In February, 1956, Stalin's ultimate successor, Nikita S. Khrushchev, in a three-hour speech to the 20th Congress of the Communist party, denounced Stalin as a tyrant, repudiated the Stalinist purges of the 1930s, and proclaimed a policy of peaceful—but competitive—coexistence with the West. The old Stalinists, notably Lavrenti P. Beria, head of the secret police, had already been purged from the government. Beria himself was executed in 1953 after an unsuccessful grab for power.

Hardly had the world's spirits begun to lift, however, when a new series of crises gripped Europe and the Middle East. In October, 1956, Hungarian students and workers revolted against the Communist regime. Soviet garrison troops, at least partly in sympathy with the Hungarian masses, withdrew from the Hungarian capital of Budapest, but seven days later, fresh Soviet occupying forces, drawn largely from behind the Urals, brutally crushed the revolt. The United States could not intervene. The Truman Doctrine did not extend behind the Iron Curtain. Beyond the question of policy lay the terrifying prospect of thermonuclear war. In 1952, the United States had successfully tested the hydrogen bomb and had begun to build up its arsenal of these awesome weapons. The Russians were less than a year behind with their H-bomb, and intercontinental ballistic delivery systems were on the horizon.

The Hungarian revolt was still in progress when flames erupted in the Middle East. The new state of Israel, smarting over growing Arab hostility and Egypt's seizure from the British of the vital Suez Canal on July 26, 1956, launched an attack on Egypt's Sinai Peninsula through the Gaza Strip. Britain and France intervened on Israel's side, and the U.N. demanded a cease-fire. The United States supported the U.N.

The year after their first political contest, Adlai E. Stevenson was the guest of honor at this White House luncheon hosted by President Eisenhower.

demand and condemned the attack, a surprising move on the surface. But the action was an expression of increasing concern by Eisenhower and Secretary of State John Foster Dulles for stability in this strategic and oil-rich region. The Arab world was being actively wooed by the Soviets. If the U.S.S.R. could establish Communist domination here, it would control one-sixth of the world's oil resources and stand athwart the gateway between Europe and the Far East. In January, 1957, President Eisenhower took steps to protect what he considered America's vital interests in the Middle East. He issued the Eisenhower Doctrine, a new policy declaring that the United States would give economic aid and would use "armed force" to protect any country in the area from Communist aggression. In May, 1958, that policy was tested when pro-Egyptian forces, backed by the Soviet Union, threatened the Lebanese government. Eisenhower ordered marines into Lebanon and kept them there at the request of the government for a full month until internal stability was restored.

Balance of terror

By this time, international peace had poised delicately for nearly a decade upon a wave of continuing crisis, and the old European imperative for peace—a balance of power—began to give way to a new concept: World peace was not only *threatened* but also *protected* by the terror of nuclear warfare. Equilibrium was being maintained, despite crises, by the unwillingness of either superpower to risk a nuclear strike; both powers feared a counterstrike. In short, there existed a balance of terror.

Beneath this fearsome umbrella the principal underlying goal of the United States, the prevention of another major war, was being achieved. The major domestic goal, prevention of another economic depression, was also weathering well. During the decade of the 1950s, the nation sustained an average economic growth rate of approximately 3.2% annually. A recession occurred in 1956–57, but pump priming by the Eisenhower administration—largely in the form of a massive federal program for building the Interstate Highway system—quickly restored the upward movement of the economy.

Eisenhower had handily won reelection in 1956, beating Adlai Stevenson again, this time by an electoral margin of 457 to 73. But for the first time in 108 years, an American President would not carry into office with him a majority in either of the two houses of Congress. The election was a tribute to the great popularity of Eisenhower the man. But new forces were stirring in the land. A new generation of leaders, "born in this century," was rising, and new national goals, concerned as much with quality as with quantity, were beginning to take form. They would give rise in time to two internal revolutions, one social, the other technological. Both of them would lead to profound changes in the America of the next decade.

COURTESY OF THE ACADEMY OF MOTION PICTURE ARTS AND SCIENCES

THAT'S ENTERTAINMENT

"Lights . . . camera . . . action!" After World War II, these words once again captured the American imagination. The public craved diversion and escape, and the entertainment industry was there to help. Movies, which had been very big business before the war, became bigger and more extravagant than ever as the motion-picture studios tried to counter the threat from the new television industry. The Academy Awards ceremony, with its small statuette, the Oscar, continued to represent the pinnacle of glamor and success in the American entertainment industry. By 1965, however, television had become the major communications medium in American life, a mirror through which Americans could see themselves as they would like to be. Throughout the postwar years, the American theater continued to provide entertainment in the form of musical comedies, and and in the late 1940s and early 1950s, new dramatists like Tennessee Williams and William Inge began to treat human behavior in new and sometimes shocking ways.

THE BROADWAY MUSICAL BRINGS DREAMS TO LIFE

My Fair Lady (1956), a Lerner and Loewe musical adapted from George Bernard Shaw's play *Pygmalion*, fulfilled the dream of every Broadway musical: it became the most successful show in Broadway history (later superseded by *A Chorus Line*) and then went on to become a blockbuster motion picture, in 1964. *Funny Girl* (1964) first brought to wide public attention the talents of the actress and singer Barbra Streisand.

COURTESY OF THE LINCOLN CENTER LIBRARY OF THE
PERFORMING ARTS, NEW YORK CITY PUBLIC LIBRARY.

DRAMATIC THEATER
EXPLORES THE AMERICAN PSYCHE

In *Summer and Smoke* (1948), Tennessee Williams continued an unbroken string of stage successes that had begun with *The Glass Menagerie* and *A Streetcar Named Desire*; this time Williams dealt with the lost dreams of spinsterhood in a small Southern town. John Van Druten's *I Am A Camera* (1951), based on the Berlin Stories of Christopher Isherwood, cast an eye back to pre-war Germany; it later became the basis for the 1970s musical *Cabaret*. William Inge set his drama *Picnic* (1953) in a small, rural American town; Edward Albee explored the underside of a "normal" American marriage in *Who's Afraid of Virginia Woolf?* (1962).

WAR AND PEACE

America's fighting men were memorialized in films like *The Sands of Iwo Jima* (1949), and John Wayne (who never served in World War II) became everyone's ideal of the tough but tender American man, while films like *The Day the Earth Stood Still* (1951) pressed the case for world peace.

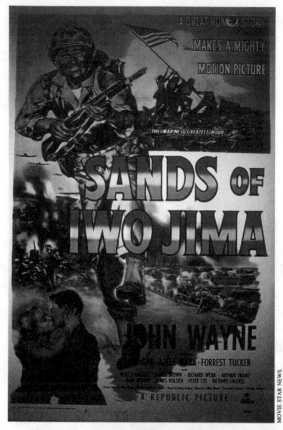

''OLD PROS'' CREATE NEW HITS

Pre-war giants like directors Howard Hawks and John Huston continued to produce box-office hits such as *Monkey Business* (1952) and *The African Queen* (1951), and veteran screen personalities such as Katharine Hepburn, Humphrey Bogart, and Cary Grant (shown here with Ginger Rogers and Harry Carey Jr.) still fascinated and delighted their movie audiences. In 1962, an ailing Columbia Pictures was saved from bankruptcy by the success of David Lean's *Lawrence of Arabia*.

MOVIE STAR NEWS.

MOVIE STAR NEWS.

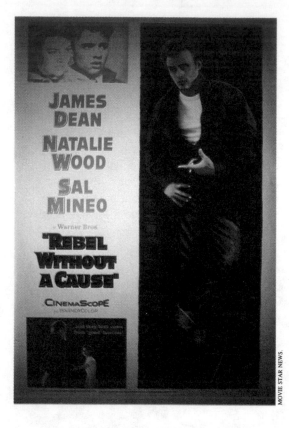

NEW STARS FOR A NEW AUDIENCE

In the 1950s, Hollywood began to target films for a new audience—the American teenager. James Dean became a star overnight as young Americans identified with his portrayals of alienation from adult America. The music and persona of Elvis Presley became a national obsession in the mid-1950s, and he appeared in films addressed to for his youthful audience.

SETTING SCREEN HISTORY TO MUSIC

MOVIE STAR NEWS.

Hollywood wrote a history of the change-over from silent movies to talkies and set it to music in *Singin' in the Rain* (1952). Gene Kelly choreographed dances that mixed ballet and modern dance with his uncanny flair for the dramatic, and with Cyd Charisse and Donald O'Connor, he created some screen history of his own.

MOVIE STAR NEWS.

HITCHCOCK, STEWART, AND CLIFT

In *Vertigo* (1958), which starred veteran actor James Stewart and newcomer Kim Novak, Alfred Hitchcock mirrored our obsession with what is versus what seems to be. Fred Zinneman's *From Here to Eternity* (1953) captured the eve of World War II and featured a cavalcade of stars including Montgomery Clift, Donna Reed, and Frank Sinatra.

MOVIE STAR NEWS.

MOVIE STAR NEWS.

HOLLYWOOD MEETS BROADWAY

Broadway moved to Hollywood with magnificent results in Charles K. Feldman's production of *A Streetcar Named Desire* (1951), directed by Elia Kazan and starring Marlon Brando and Vivien Leigh. *All About Eve* (1950), a witty, sophisticated portrayal of the world of the New York stage written and directed by Joseph Mankiewicz, starred Bette Davis (in a now-legendary screen performance), George Sanders, and Gary Merrill (shown), and featured the young Marilyn Monroe in one of her first screen roles.

MOVIE STAR NEWS.

MOVIE STAR NEWS.

HOLLYWOOD ON HOLLYWOOD

In *A Star Is Born* and *Sunset Boulevard*, Hollywood made films about itself. *A Star Is Born* (1954) is the story of the destruction of an alcoholic actor's life and career. Judy Garland and James Mason re-created roles played in the original 1937 film by Janet Gaynor and Frederic March. *Sunset Boulevard*, starring Gloria Swanson and William Holden, tells a sad tale of how Hollywood treats its has-beens and hopefuls; it is a story of what can happen to the human psyche when the cameras stop turning and the agents stop calling.

CLEOPATRA— ON SCREEN AND OFF

As television became bigger and more competitive, movie screens got larger, budgets grew bigger, and stars more glamorous and expensive. Perhaps the most lavish spectacle of them all was Walter Wanger's production of *Cleopatra* (1963), becoming one of the most expensive flops in the history of film. The film took years to make and was most notable for the off-screen romance between its two stars, Elizabeth Taylor and Richard Burton.

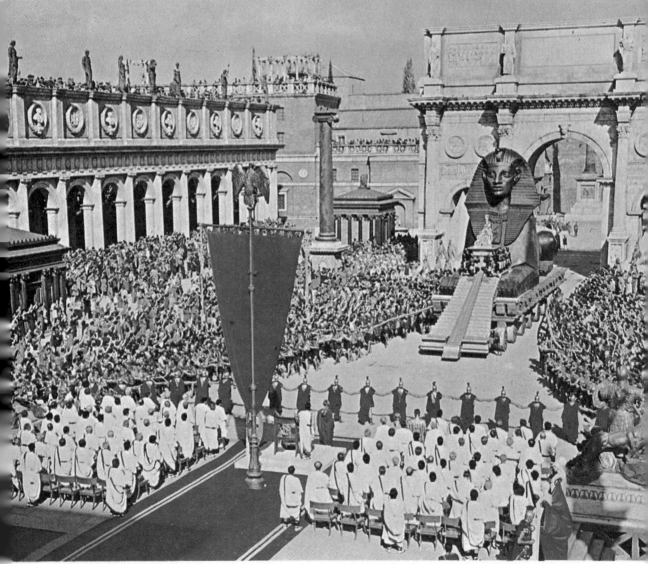

MOVIE STAR NEWS.

MARILYN . . .

MOVIE STAR NEWS.

Some Like It Hot (1959), a hilarious comedy of the Roaring Twenties, featured Jack Lemmon and Tony Curtis as a pair of musicians who put on dresses and joined an all-girl band in order to escape from the Chicago mob. The movie also starred Marilyn Monroe, who, by this time, was every man's dream girl. Appearing in films throughout the 1950s and into the early 1960s, Marilyn Monroe (shown here in a scene from *The Seven Year Itch* [1955]) embodied a vulnerability and physical attractiveness that the movie public found irresistible.

MOVIE STAR NEWS.

AMERICA EXPORTS HERSELF

The United States exported its unique postwar culture abroad through the release of American films overseas. American film stars like Rock Hudson and Marilyn Monroe were not only well known in Coffeyville, Kansas, and Medford, Oregon, they were household names in Paris, Rome, and Hong Kong, as well. American films became a powerful weapon in the Cold War, spreading American social ideals around the world.

MOVIE STAR NEWS.

MOVIE STAR NEWS.

TELEVISION— THE GREAT COMEDIANS

During the postwar era, television became the great national pastime. The talking picture box in our living rooms came to dominate our evenings, and before long, concerned critics dubbed television "the vast wasteland." The first television stars were great comedians who had made the transition to television from the radio, movies, or vaudeville. "Your Show of Shows" (1950-1954), starring Sid Caesar and Imogene Coca, became the prototype for the television comedy-variety show. "The Honeymooners," starring Jackie Gleason, Audrey Meadows, Art Carney, and Joyce Randolph, chronicled the weekly adventures of Ralph Kramden, a New York bus driver, and his hilarious neighbor Ed Norton. Without a doubt America's favorite early television show was "I Love Lucy" (1951-1961), which starred Desi Arnaz and Lucille Ball and ran for more than ten years.

THE SERIOUS
AND THE SILLY

The late 1950s also saw the rise of the one-hour dramatic series based on a central character who appeared in a different adventure each week. Among the first of these was ''Perry Mason'' (1957-1966), played by the actor Raymond Burr. Television was coming of age, and its dramatic series often dealt with current social issues such as capital punishment or free speech. Saturday mornings, however, were reserved for children, and a whole generation grew up watching Daffy Duck cartoons while eating cereal and milk.

COMEDY, ADVENTURE, AND HORSE SENSE

Television first brought comic-book characters to life in the 1965 series ''Batman'' (1965-68), which starred Adam West and Burt Ward as Batman and Robin. The series, a tongue-in-cheek comedy/adventure, featured a bevy of guest stars from Burgess Meredith to Cesar Romero. Americans still loved a good western, too, and ''Bonanza'' (1959-1973) was the most popular, following the adventures of the Cartwright family on their ranch, the Ponderosa.

Television shaped the way America saw itself: it became the national source of news and information, diversion and entertainment. By the mid-1960s, many in America were questioning the values and standards on which the postwar world was based: theatre, film, and television, of course, reflected this questioning. By then, movies and television were a permanent part of the very fabric of our lives.

COURTESY OF THE LINCOLN CENTER LIBRARY OF THE PERFORMING ARTS, NEW YORK CITY PUBLIC LIBRARY.

MOVIE STAR NEWS.

1413

CHAPTER 48

"THE TORCH HAS BEEN PASSED"

The words rang out in the chill Washington air on January 20, 1961: "The torch has been passed to a new generation of Americans—born in this century. . . ." They heralded a different kind of Presidency from the grandfatherly Eisenhower years. "Ask not what your country can do for you," Democrat John F. Kennedy demanded, "ask what you can do for your country." Kennedy made it clear that America's youngest President since Theodore Roosevelt would be "in the forefront of the battle," and he called for the involvement of the whole nation in the American enterprise. He inherited an America that had come a long way from the relative simplicities of the immediate postwar years. The technological legacy of two major wars was transforming every major sector of life—industrial, commercial, agricultural, and social. Jet transportation

Although John F. Kennedy was President for less than three years, his impact on the nation was enormous. To many he seemed to be the embodiment of revived idealism in American political leadership.

forded the oceans of the world faster than the railroads of less than 25 years before had negotiated the routes between the major cities. Television brought the events and the ideas of the entire world into the living room of the average American, informing his thinking, widening his views. Unlike the post-World War I period when America retreated into isolation, the United States was now a world leader. The nation's unparalleled economic position had much to do with the difference. The gross national product, the total value of all goods and services produced in the United States, had risen from nearly $212,000,000,000 in 1945 to more than $503,000,000,000 in 1960. Median family income stood at $5,835 for whites, $3,233 for nonwhites; household savings totaled $72,000,000,000,000; the civilian labor force reached 70,000,000—an increase of 16,000,000 jobs since the end of the war. The nation that had celebrated the virtues of the home and stability for more than a century had also developed a wanderlust. Sociologists estimated that the typical American breadwinner would change employers no less than seven times during his work life. Approxi-

The televised Kennedy-Nixon debates in 1960 helped put the lesser known Senator before the nation and established a new method of campaigning.

mately 1,000,000 families a year were moving to new parts of the country.

However, if the average American felt free to pursue his prosperous dream of a home in the suburbs, there was another American who could not. He went by many names. He was disadvantaged, with little schooling and few skills. He was numbered among the 6% of the work force that was unemployed. He was the urban poor, nesting among the rotting tenements of the big-city black ghettos. He was the semiskilled agricultural worker, displaced by farm mechanization. He was the migrant laborer, never settling long enough in one place to get his family established and his children educated. He was the low-skilled industrial worker bumped by au-

tomation. "One-third of Americans go to bed hungry each night," Kennedy had charged in his campaign against Vice-President Richard M. Nixon. "We must do better." Although the statistic was overdrawn in campaign rhetoric, the condition was not. Henceforth, the attack on both urban and rural poverty would receive priority among the nation's objectives.

Kennedy went on to defeat Nixon by the slim margin of 117,574 popular votes out of nearly 69,000,000 cast, though his electoral tally was a comfortable 303 to Nixon's 219.

In his inaugural, the new President depicted the cause of freedom as being in its hour of "maximum peril," and, mixing both domestic and foreign-policy goals, asked for the nation's support in "a struggle against the common enemies of man: tyranny, poverty, disease, and war itself." This struggle was almost immediately focused on American-Soviet relations. Kennedy was persuaded that the Soviet Union had a temporary lead over the United States in weapons technology, particularly in the development of nuclear-delivery systems. The so-called missile gap had been one of his favorite themes during the campaign. There was, moreover, ample reason to credit the U.S.S.R. with a highly developed capacity in rocketry. The Soviets had shocked the thinly financed American space establishment in the geophysical year of 1957 with the successful launching of *Sputnik I,* the first earth satellite. As a result, the United States had belatedly switched from special scientific rockets to military rockets for satellite exploration of near space, but the U.S.S.R. continued to reap prestige from an impressive array of firsts.

Unrest in the U.S.S.R

Despite the policy of "peaceful coexistence" enunciated by Soviet Chairman Khrushchev, relations between the two superpowers in 1961 were at their lowest ebb since the Stalin era. In May of the previous year, after an American U-2 spy plane had been downed inside the Soviet Union, Khrushchev had broken up a summit conference in Paris by loudly denouncing an infuriated President Eisenhower. Evidence has since accumulated that Khrushchev was acting under extreme internal pressure. He had

decided in 1954 to increase the number of acres under cultivation instead of building more fertilizer plants. The so-called virgin lands program was designed to put Soviet agriculture on an independent footing. However, by 1957, Khrushchev's agricultural policy had been defeated by the short growing season on the Russian Steppes. His determination to build a Soviet consumer society was also facing stiff opposition from those within the government who wanted to continue to build up heavy industry and export production. The spy-plane incident and the show trial of the captured pilot, Francis Gary Powers, was a tailor-made diversion for Khrushchev, whose political status at home seemed to depend on keeping international tensions at a high pitch.

Kennedy set out to reduce these tensions by gathering the loose strands of the diplomatic dialogue between the two countries, but his first year in office was a dismal one for American foreign policy. On April 12, 1961, the Soviet Union's prestige as a leading technological nation was impressively advanced with the world's first manned space orbit by Soviet Air Force Major Yuri Gagarin. Five days later, the international prestige of the United States plummeted when an American-organized and financed invasion of Cuba by anti-Communist exiles failed on the beaches of the Bay of Pigs. On June 3 and 4, the President met with Khrushchev in Vienna for a hastily arranged summit conference. He came away shocked by the Soviet leader's intransigence. In an effort to convince the Soviet Union that America was determined to support its European allies, the following month Kennedy countered a Communist proposal to make Berlin into a demilitarized "free city" by saying he would increase the size of U.S. military forces. On August 13, East Germany closed the border between East and West Berlin—first with barbed wire, then with an eight-foot-high masonry wall—to stop the flight of East Berliners to the more prosperous Western sector. The Soviet Union then began rattling its thermonuclear arsenal, setting off several hydrogen test blasts in October to demonstrate its might. The following year, Khrushchev made an offensive thrust into the Western Hemisphere that brought about the most dangerous face-off of the Cold War.

Since the abortive invasion attempt at the Bay of Pigs, the Soviet Union had been arming Cuba. The United States took the position that so long as the arms buildup on the Communist island remained defensive, there would be no interference. However, by mid-October of 1962, evidence began to accumulate that the Soviet Union was installing intermediate-range missiles in Fidel Castro's Cuba. Kennedy's response was swift. At the United Nations, U.S. Ambassador Adlai E. Stevenson presented the photographic documentation of new medium-range missile sites and dramatically challenged the Soviet Ambassador to deny it. On the military front, Kennedy put into effect a naval "quarantine" of Cuba—a selective blockade authorized to stop, search, and turn back any vessels carrying missiles. On the night of October 22, Kennedy informed the American public of his stand, and the world held its breath. The two superpowers stood like barroom fighters, "eyeball to eyeball." As a fleet of Communist merchant vessels carrying missiles on their open decks approached Cuban waters, communications between Washing-

Fidel Castro's speeches spellbound the Cubans after he came to power. But he himself was soon spellbound by Russia.

When the Soviet Union removed its missiles from Cuba in 1962, an American warship (foreground) moved alongside to inspect the deck cargo.

ton and Moscow began to carry messages from the Soviet leadership, at first denying offensive intentions in Cuba but finally agreeing to turn back the fleet. Washington made the further demand that the missiles already in Cuba be pulled out. With appropriate face-saving language, the Soviets agreed. The crisis was over.

The showdown actually resulted in more realistic relations between the two countries. The United States had demonstrated that it would not tolerate an open threat to its territory. The Soviet Union,

in effect, admitted that it had pushed too hard, and it backed off. The nature of the American military response was such that the Soviet Union could do so with some grace, and it was this carefully calculated initiative that probably saved the day. Both nations, thoroughly shaken by the close call, almost immediately reopened negotiations on a limited nuclear-test ban, and a "hot line" was installed between the White House and the Kremlin to permit instantaneous communication in times of crisis. Within a year, the United States and the Soviet

Union had worked out a pact to halt all testing in the atmosphere, under the seas, and in outer space. More than 100 other nations signed the treaty in October, 1963. France, intent on developing its own nuclear strike capacity, refused to sign, as did Red China. Nevertheless, the treaty was a substantial step toward limiting the spread of nuclear weapons. Inasmuch as the ban involved cooperative effort, it was also a step toward the easing of international tensions. Other tentative steps were being taken as well. Trade barriers with a number of the nations in Eastern Europe—first Marshal Tito's independently minded Yugoslavia, then others—were being bridged. The United States, for the first time since the war, started selling wheat directly to the Soviet Union. Cultural exchanges were being arranged, and a new mood of international understanding was beginning to prevail.

Civil rights as an issue

Meanwhile, the strings of domestic crisis were growing taut. Presented daily with the evidence of growing affluence, the black American was becoming impatient with the slowly grinding wheels of economic and social justice. Steps to correct unequal treatment of racial minorities had been in progress ever since the war. This progress was admittedly slow. In 1948, Truman, by executive order, outlawed racial segregation in the armed forces. The Federal Housing Act of 1949 forbade racial discrimination in federally financed housing. In the landmark case of *Brown* v. *Board of Educa-tion of Topeka, Kansas*, in 1954, the Supreme Court struck down the 58-year-old doctrine of "separate but equal" accommodations for white and black schoolchildren and ordered Southern school districts to integrate their classes. The federal courts later extended this doctrine to the Northern states, where, it was successfully argued, the concept of the neighborhood school district resulted in de facto segregation. The White House, Eisenhower made clear, was prepared to back the courts' decisions with direct action.

In 1957, pursuant to the Supreme Court decision, the Little Rock, Arkansas, Board of Education adopted a plan of integration that called for the admission of some black students to the city's Central High School, starting in September. As the time for the opening of school approached, Governor Orval E. Faubus declared that integration would threaten the peace. He then stationed national guard units around the high school. When nine black children attempted to enroll, Faubus ordered the national guard to keep them from enrolling in their assigned school.

Under federal injunction, the national guard was withdrawn. Then rioting mobs appeared, bent on keeping the black children from the school. At that juncture, Eisenhower ordered 1,000 federal paratroopers into the city and pressed the national guard into federal service, thereby removing it from the Governor's control. Under the protection of federal bayonets, the black children entered the school. Thus, the principle that the fed-

Earl Warren (seated, center) becomes a symbol of constitutional liberalism as Chief Justice. Above is the "Warren Court" as it looked after 1962.

eral government would not tolerate any local defiance of court orders on integration was established.

There were some federal actions on behalf of civil rights besides those taken by the courts. In 1957, Congress passed the Civil Rights Act, the first significant legislation in the field since Reconstruction. It created a federal Civil Rights Commission and gave the government new power to seek injunctions against interference with black voting.

Much of the impetus toward faster desegregation, however, came from the blacks themselves, together with some supporting whites. In 1960, a group of black students entered a department store in Greensboro, North Carolina, and sat quietly at the lunch counter to protest the fact that blacks were not served there. This was the beginning of the "sit-in" movement that spread quickly through the South and resulted in the desegregation of several lunch counters and public waiting rooms. A year later, some black organizations started the practice of "freedom rides"—blacks and whites riding through the South and entering "white" waiting rooms. Many of the sit-in demonstrators and freedom riders were arrested, and some were attacked; but they succeeded in quickening the pace of desegregation.

As the pace quickened, resistance in many parts of the country stiffened. In 1962–63, the governors of both Alabama

1421

*In 1965, Martin Luther King led 25,000 marchers from Selma to Montgom-
ery, Alabama. Ralph Bunche is on Dr. King's right; Mrs. King is on his left.*

and Mississippi attempted to prevent
blacks from enrolling in their respective
state universities. As a result, national
guard troops, activated by President
Kennedy, had to be employed to quell
violent riots. In Birmingham, Alabama,
a protest march led by the Reverend Dr.
Martin Luther King, Jr., was interrupted
by Police Commissioner Eugene ''Bull''

Connor, who unleashed a pack of police
dogs on the marchers and jailed Dr.
King. A church in Birmingham was
bombed, killing four young black girls
and maiming several other black children. On the very night that President
Kennedy, in a televised speech, called
for a settlement of the ''moral issue'' of
racial injustice, Medgar Evers, Missis-

sippi chief of the National Association for the Advancement of Colored People, was assassinated in Jackson.

On June 19, 1963, Kennedy sent the strongest civil-rights bill in history to Congress. The bill called for a public-accommodations section, which would make it illegal to discriminate in public facilities, grant the Attorney General authority to file suit where school desegregation had not been carried out, assure fair employment and voter-registration practices, and withhold federal funds from projects in which discrimination is practiced. When it became apparent that Congressional action was not going to be as swift as had been hoped, black leaders announced plans for a march on Washington. Kennedy was apprehensive. If fewer than the estimated 100,000 marchers should show up, he reasoned, Congress might feel that passage of the bill was not urgent. However, on August 28, 1963, more than 250,000 black and white Americans converged on Washington and heard Dr. King describe his dream "that one day on the red hills of Georgia the sons of former slaves and

The Lincoln Memorial was the focal point for blacks and whites at the historic civil-rights Freedom March on Washington on August 28, 1963.

sons of former slaveowners will be able to sit down together at the table of brotherhood.''

The President is slain

Then, abruptly, the unthinkable occurred. President John F. Kennedy was fatally shot in Dallas, Texas, on November 22, 1963. Not since McKinley's death in 1901 had an American President been assassinated. Kennedy, whose identification with civil-rights causes had made him a target of right-wing extremists and Southern conservatives, had been mending political fences in the key state of Texas. Paradoxically, he was slain by a young left-wing fanatic, Lee Harvey Oswald. Oswald was arrested that afternoon and two days later was himself fatally shot by a Dallas nightclub owner, Jack Ruby, while being escorted through a corridor by Dallas policemen. The shock waves spread around the world. Kennedy had made the young his special constituency. Not only young people, but also young nations identified their interests with his, and his Presidency had done much to restore a sense of the nation's ideals both at home and abroad.

By the millions, young and old alike mourned him around the world. America rallied to bury its murdered President with ceremonies of dignity and honor, and efficiently transferred power to the new President, Lyndon B. Johnson. As Johnson told Congress, "This is our challenge—not to hesitate, not to pause, not to turn about and linger over this evil moment but to continue on our course so that we may fulfill the destiny that history has set for us."

Johnson entered the White House aware that he would not fall undisputed heir to the loyalty Kennedy commanded from the powerful liberal wing of the Democratic party. Yet he needed this loyalty if he were to reanimate the old Democratic coalition originally constructed by his Presidential model, Franklin D. Roosevelt. Both Kennedy and Johnson had sensed, in 1960, that the nation needed new goals. Kennedy spoke to this need, in 1961, when he set the space program on its course to the moon. Both addressed themselves to these goals in their many expressions on the quality of American life and the gaps that had opened between the comfortable majority and the deprived minorities. Johnson would need his whole party behind him if he were to be effective in setting the nation on a new course. He therefore was determined to push Kennedy's domestic program through Congress.

The Johnson approach

One of the most experienced politicians ever to reach the Presidency, Johnson was an altogether different sort of man from Kennedy. He was an expert in the arts of negotiating and bargaining. Combining his own skills with the will-

John F. Kennedy was the fourth American President to be killed by an assassin's bullet. While the world wept, his coffin lay in state in the Capitol Rotunda.

1424

ingness of most Congressmen to build a legislative memorial to Kennedy, Johnson energetically engineered a spectacular series of legislative successes. The Civil Rights Act of 1964, which had been languishing in committee since Kennedy's proposal, and a tax cut—to name the most significant of his many achievements—were quickly enacted into law during Johnson's first year in office.

While Johnson's record in Congress had been generally conservative, he had, as Vice-President, worked tirelessly to advance the liberal causes of the Kennedy administration. As President, however, he announced that he would seek a national consensus, that he intended to be the President of all the people. He began by declaring war on poverty in America.

Built around the Office of Economic Opportunity, Johnson's antipoverty measures provided for, among other things, a domestic peace corps known as VISTA (Volunteers in Service to America); a Job Corps for teaching vocational skills to disadvantaged young Americans; a Neighborhood Youth Corps to reach the street gangs of the big cities; plus a number of other assistance measures for farmers, migrant workers, small businessmen, and undereducated adults. Later, a Model Cities program was added to provide tangible examples of urban residential reconstruction. The legislative performance was truly remarkable. Johnson had wrung from a Congress that was as reluctant as those that had blocked the domestic programs of two prior Democratic Presidents, a summary expression of unprecedented national goals: end poverty, eliminate racial, economic, and educational discrimination, halt urban decay—right away!

These remarkable goals proved easier to express in law than to accomplish in fact. From the start, with rare exception, the new poverty programs ran into administrative and executive problems and sectional and local resistance. Americans began to wonder whether Johnson's bright vision of "The Great Society could really be achieved."

Yet, as America moved into the election year of 1964, the Johnson administration—its legislative successes still largely untarnished—was clearly in the ascendant. With the exception of the Deep South, Johnson's party had not appeared more unified since the Roosevelt era. Johnson's nomination was only a formality. The Republicans nominated Arizona Senator Barry M. Goldwater, a conservative. The Democrats immediately set out to show that Goldwater was even more conservative than his own party believed him to be, and the G.O.P. candidate did little to combat this impression. It was Goldwater's belief that the millions of Americans who did not vote in Presidential elections—sometimes as much as 40% of the electorate—abstained because both parties in recent years had chosen liberal candidates for the Presidency. Goldwater hoped to entice this silent vote into a new coalition.

He saw the nation facing two clear ideological choices—left or right—and he was determined to offer his candidacy as "a choice, not an echo."

Johnson, however, refused to follow Goldwater's scenario. He believed that the typical American would identify with moderate sentiments. The President's choice of the middle ground frustrated the Republican campaign strategists. Presented with a Republican candidate effectively depicted as "extreme," the American voters went to the polls and proved Johnson's assessment of the public mind overwhelmingly correct. He won the Presidency in his own right with 486 electoral votes to Goldwater's 52. In the process, his party strengthened its hold on the Congress by one seat in the Senate and 37 in the House. A President so mandated and so endowed might have looked forward to a term of high accomplishment. But a land mine awaited Lyndon Baines Johnson in Southeast Asia.

Vice-President Humphrey and President Johnson together at the White House.

John F. Kennedy, Twenty Years Later

A SPECIAL CONTRIBUTION BY
WILLIAM E. LEUCHTENBURG

Two decades after Kennedy's death, historians were still not sure whether he was one of our best Presidents, or "an optical illusion," "an expensively programmed waxwork."

The murder of John F. Kennedy occasioned an overwhelming sense of grief that may be without parallel in our history. When the news first was announced, people wept openly in the streets, and during the painful weekend that followed, as the mesmerizing images of the youthful President and his family were flashed again and again on the television screens, the feeling of deprivation deepened. A San Francisco columnist reported: "It is less than 72 hours since the shots rang out in Dallas, yet it seem a lifetime—a lifetime of weeping skies, wet eyes and streets. . . . Over the endless weekend, San Francisco looked like a city that was only slowly emerging from a terrible bombardment. Downtown, on what would normally have been a bustling Saturday, the people walked slowly, as

in shock, their faces pale and drawn, their mood as somber as the dark clothes they wore under the gray skies."

To the slain President's admirers and associates, his death signified not merely a cruel personal loss but the end of an era. "For all of us, life goes on—but brightness has fallen from the air," observed his special counsel Theodore Sorensen. "A Golden age is over and it will never be again." One of Kennedy's earliest biographers, William Manchester, had jotted down on the morning of Kennedy's Inauguration the words of the sixteenth-century martyr, Hugh Latimer. "We shall this day light such a candle by God's grace . . . as I trust shall never be put out." "Now," Manchester wrote, "the light was gone from our lives, and I was left to grope in the darkness of the dead past." At the United Nations, Ambassador Adlai Stevenson rose to say, "We will bear the grief of his death to the day of ours."

Yet the mourning for Kennedy was by no means limited to his circle; it was felt no less deeply by those who had been his critics and adversaries. Few had commented more caustically on the New Frontier than Norman Mailer. But Mailer now declared: "What one has written about Kennedy was not reverent. Now, in the wake of the President's assassination, a sense of real woe intrudes itself. For it may be that John F. Kennedy's best claim to greatness was that he made an atmosphere possible in which one could be critical of him, biting, whimsical, disrespectful, imaginative, even out of line. It was the first

President Kennedy confers with his younger brother Robert, who in 1963 became the first brother of a president to serve as Attorney General.
JOHN F. KENNEDY LIBRARY

1429

time in America's history that one could mock the Presidency on so high a level, and we may have to live for half a century before such a witty and promising atmosphere exists again.'' Nor was Mailer alone. In Guinea, Skou Tour stated, ''I have lost my only true friend in the outside world,'' and in Algiers, Ben Bella, his voice breaking, said, ''I can't believe it. Believe me, I'd rather it happen to me than to him.''

Such expressions were not atypical but representative, for the most conspicuous aspect of the anguish over the assassination was its worldwide character. In London more than a thousand traveled from distant parts of the city to pay homage at the U.S. Embassy in Grosvenor Square, and the same instinct drew mourners to the American missions in Moscow and in Cairo, in Madras and in Tananarive. On the hillsides in Kampala by the residence of the American envoy, Ugandans sat in a silent vigil. From Yokohama a correspondent wrote: "Immediately when there came the news of Mr. Kennedy's death, there was a silencing of life here and then a siege of grief as I have never seen before and never thought possible in Japan. No one told the Japanese to be shocked: they just cried with pain and anger and sorrow, as if the human psyche had been slammed in a car door, and maimed.''

In Britain the BBC's "That Was The Week That Was,'' a program distinguished by its impiety toward authority, called Kennedy ''the first Western politician to make politics a respectable profession for thirty years,'' and in the *Manchester Guardian Weekly,* David Gourlay went so far as to say, ''For the first time in my life I think I know how the disciples must have felt when Jesus was crucified.''

In the United States historians were not immune from such sentiments, though they were inclined to be more restrained. Even in 1963 they were reluctant to subscribe to the sentiment revealed by *Public Opinion Quarterly,* which found that ''a full half of the adult population'' in America judged Kennedy to be ''one of the two or three best Presidents the country ever had.'' Yet a good many historians were disposed to give him good marks. James MacGregor Burns, who had taken a detached view of Kennedy in his exemplary campaign biography, concluded that, as a dramatizer of issues, Kennedy rated with Lincoln, while Arthur Link, author of the definitive multivolume

life of Woodrow Wilson, observed that Kennedy brought to the White House ''qualities of vigor, rationality, and noble vision matched only by Theodore Roosevelt, Woodrow Wilson, and Franklin Roosevelt in this century. It is too early to try to fix his place among the Presidents, but I am inclined to believe that historians will rank him as a great President.''

Twenty years after Kennedy's death, historians were far from reaching a consensus on his brief Presidency, but few would be disposed to rank him so highly. The imagery associated with the name *Kennedy,* so brightly burnished in 1963, has tarnished. Kennedy's reputation has been deflated by what one writer called ''a group of late-souring historians known collectively as the revisionists,'' and even those who had once been well disposed toward him have had second thoughts. Asked in 1973 whether his view of Kennedy had changed in the past decade, Arthur Link replied: ''I should say that I somewhat overrated his abilities, his vision. . . . As we look back on the years '61 to '63, what seemed like great events and forward movement don't seem so great and so forward now.''

A sense of disappointment in Kennedy was already a familiar theme in 1963. It had been voiced frequently while Kennedy was alive, by liberals as well as by conservatives. ''Washington under Kennedy, somehow, isn't the way we thought it would be,'' wrote *The New Republic's* ''TRB'' six months before the assassination. ''Somehow, we felt Mr. Kennedy would do more.'' From the Right had come Victor Lasky's vitriolic best seller, *J.F.K.: The Man and the Myth,* of which one reviewer said, ''Mr. Lasky knows how to use the knee.'' Lasky maintained that ''Kennedy did not appear to know where he was going—or what he was doing.''

In the years since 1963 some writers have carried this criticism to the point of saying that Kennedy's place in history has altogether vanished. In England, Malcolm Muggeridge wrote, ''John F. Kennedy, it is now coming to be

The President and his family are seen here before Easter Sunday Mass while vacationing at the Kennedy family compound in Palm Beach, Florida. Pictured are Jacqueline Bouvier Kennedy, John F. Kennedy, Jr., the President and his daughter Caroline.

Outside the Executive Office Building at the White House, President Kennedy confers with Robert S. McNamara, Secretary of Defense from 1961 to 1967.

realized, was a nothing-man—an expensively programmed waxwork; a camera-microphone-public relations creation whose career, on examination, turns into a strip cartoon rather than history.'' From a more radical perspective, I.F. Stone said of Kennedy in 1973, ''by now he is simply an optical illusion.'' Even someone as well disposed toward Kennedy as his former adviser, Richard Neustadt, observed sadly: ''He will be just a flicker, forever clouded by the record of his successors. I don't think history will have much space for John Kennedy.''

Commentators frequently struck this melancholy chord, for Kennedy was perceived to be a man whose career was cut short before he could prove himself. ''What was killed in Dallas was not only the President but the promise,'' wrote James Reston. ''The heart of the Kennedy legend is what might have been.'' Such expressions of sorrow implied that Kennedy had not lived long enough to accomplish much. Even those who spoke well of him often had less to say about what he had achieved than about his ''style.''

The contention that Kennedy's Presidency was inconsequential was disputed by the first authors to write at length about the thousand days— Arthur Schlesinger, Jr., and Theodore Sorensen,

each of whom had served on the White House staff. Each was impatient with the emphasis of other writers on Kennedy's style, for that suggested that he was wanting in substance. ''That special Kennedy quality that some called by the superficial name of 'style' was in reality his insistence on excellence,'' Sorensen maintained. Each claimed, too, that it was unfair to compare Kennedy's brief tenure with the much longer reign of other Presidents. Schlesinger wrote: ''He had had so little time: it was as if Jackson had died before the nullification controversy . . . as if Lincoln had been killed six months after Gettysburg . . . ''

Schlesinger and Sorensen also emphasized that, relative to other Presidents, Kennedy operated in inhospitable circumstances. Unlike predecessors who could claim overwhelming mandates for change, Kennedy had won the narrowest victory of any Presidential candidate in this century, a reality he always carried with him. A short time before his death he commented on a White House aide whom the press described as coruscatingly brilliant. ''Those guys should never forget, 50,000 votes the other way and we'd all be coruscatingly stupid.'' The same election that had given him his razor-thin victory had added twenty-one Republicans to the House and one to the Senate; he had to contend with a bipartisan conservative coalition that had balked most efforts at reform for almost a quarter-century. In 1962 alone that coalition defeated Medicare, aid to colleges, a civil rights measure, and a proposal for a new department on urban affairs. (Kennedy's critics conceded these handicaps but said he was too easily awed by them, too unwilling to risk his prestige. "In his relations with Congress," the constitutional scholar John Roche has written, "Kennedy suffered from what Soren Kierkegaard once called the 'paralysis of knowledge.' He was temperamentally incapable of leading lost causes, or causes which seemed lost in a rational appraisal of the odds.") Not only Schlesinger and Sorensen but other Kennedy champions, both in his White House years and subsequently, pointed out that there was not in the early sixties a national mood of urgency of the sort induced by the Great Depression. "There is evidence on every hand," wrote the Washington commentator Richard Rovere in 1963, "that the country fails to share Mr. Kennedy's alarm over the disorders he would like to remedy." Critics said that the apathy resulted in good part from the President's failure to arouse the people, but at the same time the essayist Andrew Hacker did not see much point "in exhorting a self-satisfied public to a state of mind it does not care to embrace."

Lastly, Kennedy's defenders argued that the President was just beginning to come into his own in his third year in office and that his great period of accomplishment lay just ahead. "My own feeling, and it can be only a feeling," reflected Clinton Rossiter, a political scientist, "is that his victories, which might have elevated him to historical greatness, were just over the next rise." Some implied that the promised land would have been occupied before Kennedy's term was out. More common is the judgment that Kennedy was building a firm base in his first term; that he would have overwhelmed Barry Goldwater in 1964, as Johnson did; and that his big triumphs would have come in his second term.

Not content with citing this range of extenuating circumstances, Kennedy's admirers claimed that the President, despite his brief tenure, had compiled a solid record of accomplishment. For instance, in his massive biography, *Kennedy,* published in 1965, Sorensen provided a detailed appendix cataloging the legislative achievements of the Eighty-sixth and Eighty-seventh Congresses. The fifteen items and twenty-one subtopics ranged from trade expansion to public works, from mental retardation to the Communications Satellite Act. To this list of accomplishments, he might have added any number of executive actions—the showdowns with Governors Ross Barnett in Mississippi and George Wallace in Alabama, the steel-price confrontation with the U.S. Steel board chairman Roger Blough, and a cluster of excellent appointments like those of Wilbur Cohen as assistant secretary of Health, Education and Welfare and Walter Heller as chairman of the Council of Economic Advisers. He also appointed some first-rate ambassadors to nations of the Third World. That same year, Schlesinger, in *A Thousand Days,* summed up the case for Kennedy's historical significance: "Yet he had accomplished so much: the new hope for peace on earth, the elimination of nuclear testing in the atmosphere and the abolition of nuclear diplomacy, the new policies toward Latin America and the Third World, the reordering of American defense, the emancipation of the American Negro, the revolution in national economic policy, the concern for poverty, the stimulus to the arts, the fight for reason against extremism and mythology."

Schlesinger's categories set the agenda for much of the subsequent controversy, not least his claim that Kennedy brought about the "emancipation of the American Negro." A great many writers, notably Howard Zinn and Victor Navasky, sharply challenged this contention. They pointed out that Kennedy moved more slowly than a tortoise in his first two years in office. He refused to propose civil rights legislation, named Southern white racists to the federal bench, and tried to stifle protest. Even in 1963, it has been said, he acted only when he was compelled to, and still too timidly.

Schlesinger's other assertions with respect to domestic affairs—especially the "revolution in national economic policy" and the "concern for poverty"—raised the question of how much should be credited to Kennedy, how much to Johnson. Kennedy's critics have said that, at the time of his death, his program was hopelessly bogged down in Congress, but that within months of taking office Johnson was able to put through a tax cut, the 1964 Civil Rights Act, and the War on Poverty. On the other hand, Kennedy partisans have claimed that both the civil rights and tax-cut measures were assured of passage in November, 1963, and that Johnson's War on Poverty was no more than a consolidation of Kennedy proposals under an exaggerated title. This conflict is not easily resolved, for the evidence can be interpreted either way. Moreover, the matter has one poignant aspect: Johnson succeeded, in part, because of the wave of grief and remorse that followed Kennedy's death.

The obverse side of the claim that Kennedy deserves credit for the advances of the 1960s is the contention that he deserves the blame for all that has gone wrong since 1963, and in the recent period, a number of historians have said that the Kennedy experience was malevolent. In *Cold War and Counterrevolution,* Richard J. Walton has written, "As Congressman and Senator, Kennedy was never a liberal, and as President, he prosecuted the Cold War more vigorously, and thus more dangerously, than did Eisenhower and Dulles." Critics have traced to Kennedy not just the vicissitudes of the Johnson administration, especially the Vietnam quagmire, but the disasters of the Nixon government too. They are distressed by the linkage of the Watergate burglars to the Bay of Pigs but even more by the overblown style of the Presidency that Kennedy bequeathed to his successors.

Kennedy's critics portray him as an implacable Cold Warrior. Of the President's Inaugural address, the British commentator Henry Fairlie has written: "These are the words which many of those who applauded the speech at the time now find offensive; and they are offensive. By what right does the leader of any free people commit them—for it was a commitment which he was making—'to pay *any* price, bear *any* burden, meet *any* hardship,' when their country is not even at war, and not directly threatened?" Kennedy then went on to point out in that address that "the graves of young Americans who answered the call to service surround the globe." Once in office, Fairlie observes, Kennedy appointed to key positions men who "seemed like hardened missiles . . . called from the Cold War silos in which they had been emplaced a decade earlier."

These Cold Warriors, as well as the President himself, are blamed for what are regarded as the administration's disastrous policies toward Cuba. The Bay of Pigs operation has almost no defenders, but objection to Kennedy's Cuban policy does not stop there. In some accounts of the missile crisis of 1962, it is not Kennedy but Khrushchev who emerges as the hero, and the President is condemned for recklessly endangering the lives of millions of innocents.

A good many writers also place the blame for the American involvement in Vietnam on Kennedy. They assert that the crucial decision to expand the war came not under Johnson but under Kennedy, that a speech he delivered at a Fort Worth breakfast on the day of his death bragged that he had "increased our special counter-insurgency forces which are engaged now in South Vietnam by 600 percent." They note, too, that the escalation under Johnson was carried out by Kennedy legatees like Dean Rusk, Robert McNamara, Walt Rostow, and McGeorge Bundy, "the best and the brightest." It was Kennedy, they say, who became intoxicated with the possibilities of counter-insurgency and left Johnson the legacy that Vietnam was a domino that must not fall.

In a 1970 article in the *New York Review of Books* with the symptomatic title "The Kennedy Fantasy," the biographer Ronald Steel recapitulated the argument of the critics: "As the brief reign of John F. Kennedy recedes into the historical past, leaving the Vietnam War as its permanent monument, . . . it is sometimes hard to remember what the Kennedy legend is all about. . . . It got tarnished somewhere around the Bay of Pigs and never recaptured its former glow. That fiasco was followed by the failure of summit diplomacy at Vienna, the manipulation of public anxiety over Berlin, a dramatic jump in the arms race, the unnecessary trip to the brink during the Cuban missile crisis, timidity on civil rights, legislative stalemate in Congress, and the decision to send the first American troops to Vietnam. Somehow everything went wrong, and increasingly, the crusading knight gave way to the conventional politician who had no answers for us. John F. Kennedy's assassination came almost as a reprieve, forever enshrining him in history as the glamorous, heroic leader he wanted to be, rather than as the politician buffeted by events he could not control."

Yet even if Kennedy has fallen in esteem since

President Kennedy strikes a stern pose with General Secretary Khrushchev at their meeting in Vienna in June, 1961, at which they discussed the growing danger of a superpower confrontation over the Berlin Wall.

1963, not all writers agree with this strongly negative assessment. Kennedy, they point out, was the first to raise issues that had been too long buried, the first to assail the verities of the Cold War and the myths of economic orthodoxy and of racism. On three successive days in June 1963, the historian William Chafe points out, Kennedy advocated new departures on world peace, economic growth, and civil rights. Though they acknowledge Kennedy's shortcomings with regard to the black revolution, historians such as Carl Brauer and Steven Lawson, after exhaustive examination of manuscript materials in the Kennedy Library and other archives, have also emphasized more positive developments, such as the expansion of black suffrage under the prodding of the Justice Department. Kennedy, concludes Brauer, both encouraged and responded to black aspirations and led the nation into its "Second Reconstruction."

Some historians have offered a spirited rebuttal, too, to the allegation that Kennedy was an implacable Cold Warrior. They point out that as early as 1961 he was saying, "the United States is neither omnipotent nor omniscient . . . we cannot impose our will upon the other 94 percent of mankind." They note, also, how often he showed restraint— in resisting loud demands to smash the Berlin Wall, in accepting compromise on Laos, in taking pains not to discomfort Khrushchev unnecessarily in the missile crisis. "Most conspicuous," wrote the critic Hannah Arendt, ". . . were the extremes to which he did *not* go." The historian Henry Pachter, who was critical of much of the President's performance, stated, "Kennedy's true claim to fame in matters of foreign policy is his genuine reversal of American attitudes to the Third World," especially in encouraging acceptance of neutralism and socialism and in taking "long shots" on "unsafe leaders" like Nkrumah. If the Alliance for Progress was flawed, it nonetheless represented a new attitude. Kennedy is perceived as an innovator who established the Peace Corps, which sent volunteers from Togo to Sarawak; negotiated the Test Ban Treaty, a first step—in his words—toward getting "the genie

President John F. Kennedy rides through Berlin with Chancellor Conrad Adenauer and Mayor Willy Brandt in June, 1961.

back in the bottle''; and set up the hotline between the Pentagon and the Kremlin. (It was first tested while Kennedy was in office, and a puzzled Russian operator replied, ''Please explain what is meant by a quick brown fox jumping over a lazy dog.'') His defenders claim either that Kennedy had already made plans to withdraw from Vietnam or that, given what one knows about him, it is unreasonable to assume that he would have persisted as Johnson did. ''He would have understood the opposition to the war as it arose,'' the *New York Times* columnist Anthony Lewis has written, ''and he would not have let his own ego get in the way of adjusting to the country's deepening perception.'' Finally, his proponents note that his American University speech in June, 1963, departed abruptly from the rhetoric of the Cold War. ''For, in the final analysis,'' Kennedy said, ''our most basic common link is that we all inhabit this small planet. We all breathe the same air. We all cherish our children's future. And we are all mortal.''

Perhaps the most judicious appreciation of Kennedy has come from a man who might have been expected to have been a critic, the socialist Michael Harrington, who said in 1973: ''The claim I make for his historic significance is both restrained and major. Within the limits of the possible, as defined by his own pragmatic liberalism and the reactionary congressional power

arrayed against it, he developed to a surprising degree. How far he would have gone, we will never know. John F. Kennedy . . . must be judged not as a shining knight nor as a failed hero but as a man of his time and place. . . . He was not, of course, a radical and it is silly to accuse him, as some of his disillusioned followers have, of not having carried out basic transformations of the system. That was never his intention, and had it been, the people would not have elected him President.

''And yet, within the context of his political and personal limitations, John F. Kennedy grew enormously. He arrived at the White House a young, and not terribly distinguished, Senator from the Eisenhower years with a tiny margin of victory and a Dixiecrat-Republican majority against him in the Congress.

''The America which inaugurated him in January, 1961, still believed in the verities of the Cold War (as did Kennedy in his speech of that day), in the sanctity of the balanced budget, and it had not begun to come to terms with that great mass movement led by Martin Luther King, Jr. The America which mourned John F. Kennedy in November, 1963, was different. It was not transformed—but it was better. That was Kennedy's modest and magnificent achievement.''

In the years to come, historians, while continuing to refine their estimates of Kennedy, will probably conclude that there is more to the history of this time than deciding whether Kennedy deserves to be admitted to the Valhalla of "Great Presidents," assigned to the vestibule of the "near great" or shoved into more crowded quarters with all the rest.

The subject invites the attention of the social historian and the cultural historian. William Carleton has reflected on Kennedy as a romantic hero: "Strange that he should have come out of the America of the machine and mass production. Or is it? People in our prosaic age, particularly young Americans, were yearning for a romantic hero, as the James Dean cult among our youth reveals. Now they have an authentic one."

Historians of religion may well explore the significance of the incumbency of the first President of the Roman Catholic faith, in particular, how it was related to the ecumenical spirit of the 1960s. One would like to know, too, what impact Kennedy may have had on the process of self-examination within the Catholic Church, though, as Schlesinger notes, the President "lived far away from the world of the Holy Name Societies, Knights of Columbus and communion breakfasts." When, in 1960, he was criticized in some Catholic quarters for insisting he was not under papal authority, he remarked, "Now I understand why Henry the Eighth set up his own church." As President, he came out against federal aid to parochial schools and commented: "As all of you know, some circles invented the myth that after Al Smith's defeat in 1928, he sent a one-word telegram to the Pope: 'Unpack.' After my press conference on the school bill, I received a one-word wire from the Pope: 'Pack.' " At a Gridiron Club affair, he added, "I asked the Chief Justice tonight whether he thought our new education bill was constitutional and he said, 'It's clearly constitutional—it hasn't got a prayer.' " And to friends at a dinner party he expressed doubt, whimsically, that Pope John was as great a figure as the press touted him to be. "You Protestants are always building him up," he said. Kennedy's detachment and his adroit wit go far toward explaining why alarm over a Catholic in the White House, so pervasive in 1960, had so largely abated by 1963, that it appears now to have been removed as a serious handicap for a Presidential aspirant, a development whose benefits may extend to other minority groups.

However, in the end, the efforts of the historians are not likely to have a very considerable effect on Kennedy's reputation, for he has already become part, not of history, but of myth, a myth that much of the public embraced and historians could not altogether escape. As Theodore White has observed: "More than any other President since Lincoln, John F. Kennedy has become myth. The greatest President in the stretch between them was, of course, Franklin D. Roosevelt; but it was difficult to make myth of Franklin Roosevelt, the country squire, the friendly judge, the approachable politician, the father figure. Roosevelt was a great man because he understood his times, and because almost always, at the historic intersections, he took the fork in the road that proved to be correct. He was so right and so strong, it was sport to challenge him. But Kennedy was cut off at the promise, not after the performance, and so it was left to television and his widow, Jacqueline, to frame the man as legend." The legend did not take long to evolve. By the time of the first anniversary of his death, *Newsweek* was remarking, "In the bare space of a year . . . Mr. Kennedy had been transfigured from man into myth—an enshrinement that would have pained him to see," and the columnist James Reston concluded, "Deprived of the place he sought in history, he has been given in compensation a place in legend."

The mythmakers focused on Kennedy as Romantic hero, in part, because Kennedy sometimes perceived himself in this manner. After his death his widow remarked: "Once . . . I thought history was something that bitter old men wrote. But then I realized history made Jack what he was. You must think of him as this little boy, sick so much of the time, reading in bed, reading history, reading the Knights of the Round Table, reading Marlborough. For Jack, history was full of heroes." In his very first race for Congress in 1946, Kennedy would tell his boon companion Dave Powers: "Years from now you can say you were with me on Saint Crispin's Day. We few, we happy few, we band of brothers." Perhaps not everything that Powers remembers occurred quite as he recounts it, but the story gains credence from the fact that Kennedy did know the Saint Crispin's Day passage from Shakespeare's *Henry V* by heart, and during a performance by Basil Rathbone at the White House, the President's only request was for that speech. Benjamin Bradlee noted that he "had a Walter Mitty streak in him, as wide as his smile. On the golf course, when he was winning, he reminded himself most of Arnold Palmer in raw power, or Julius Boros in finesse. When he was losing, he was 'the old warrior' at the end of a brilliant career, asking only that his faithful caddy point him in the right direction, and let instinct take over."

The chivalric imagery was fostered, too, by his survivors, especially by his widow. The mode was set by the elaborate state funeral that she arranged—the riderless charger with reversed boots, the tolling bells, the relentless rolls of the drums, the Black Watch Pipers, the queen of Greece and the king of the Belgians and the emperor of Ethiopia and the majestic Charles de Gaulle striding up Connecticut Avenue, and, finally, as the cortege ended its long journey, Jacqueline, bending with a torch to light the eternal flame. "It was a day," wrote Mary

President Kennedy's son John, Jr. salutes as the casket of his slain father is placed on a horse-drawn caisson outside St. Matthew's Cathedral in Washington, D.C., before the funeral procession to Arlington National Cemetery.

McGrory, "of such endless fitness, with so much pathos and panoply, so much grief nobly borne."

As important as this occasion was in establishing the romantic legend, Jacqueline Kennedy contributed even more in a subsequent interview with Theodore White. She told him: "At night, before we'd go to sleep, Jack liked to play some records; and the song he loved most came at the very end of this record. The lines he loved to hear were: *Don't let it be forgot, that once there was a spot, for one brief shining moment that was known as Camelot.*" She emphasized: "There'll be great Presidents again—and the Johnsons are wonderful, they've been wonderful to me—but there'll never be another Camelot again." The rubric *Camelot* quickly made its way into the historical literature. Indeed, Samuel Eliot Morison ended his 1965 chronicle *The Oxford History of the American People* with the lyrics from the Loewe-Lerner musical, including the words: "That once there was a fleeting wisp of glory— called Camelot."

It is unlikely that historians will ever again give so much credence to the conception of Camelot, but Kennedy's place in our history as the romantic hero, cruelly slain in his prime, seems secure. As the columnist Gerald Johnson observed: "Logical analysis will certainly be applied to Kennedy's career, and will have about as much effect on his position in history as Mrs. Partington's mop had upon the Atlantic tide. . . . Historians may protest, logicians may rave, but they cannot alter the fact that any kind of man, once touched by romance, is removed from all categories and is comparable only with the legendary. . . . Already it has happened to two of the 35 men who have held the Presidency, rendering them incapable of analysis by the instruments of scholarship; and now Washington, the god-like, and Lincoln, the saintly, have been joined by Kennedy, the Young Chevalier."

Like the fair youth on Keats's Grecian urn, Kennedy will be forever in pursuit, forever unfulfilled, but also "for ever young," beyond the power of time and the words of historians.

William E. Leuchtenburg is William Rand Kenan, Professor of History at the University of North Carolina at Chapel Hill and author of In the Shadow of FDR: From Harry Truman to Ronald Reagan.

Volume 16
ENCYCLOPEDIC SECTION

The two-page reference guide below lists the entries by categories. The entries in this section supplement the subject matter covered in the text of this volume. A **cross-reference** (*see*) means that a separate entry appears elsewhere in this section. However, certain important persons and events mentioned here have individual entries in the Encyclopedic Sections of other volumes. Consult the Index in Volume 18.

AMERICAN PRESIDENTS, STATESMEN AND POLITICIANS

Dean Acheson
Thomas E. Dewey
Everett M. Dirksen
William O. Douglas
John Foster Dulles
Dwight D. Eisenhower
James Vincent Forrestal
J. Edgar Hoover
Carey Estes Kefauver
John F. Kennedy

Joseph McCarthy
Robert S. McNamara
Adam Clayton Powell, Jr.
Samuel T. Rayburn
Dean Rusk
Adlai E. Stevenson
Robert A. Taft
Harry S. Truman
Earl Warren

CIVIL RIGHTS

Mary McLeod Bethune
Ralph Bunche

Civil-Rights Movement
Jackie Robinson

THE COLD WAR

Bay of Pigs Invasion
Berlin Airlift
Fidel Castro
Alger Hiss
The Hollywood Ten
North Atlantic Treaty Organization

Nuclear Testing
Rosenberg Spy Case
Southeast Asia Treaty Organization
Truman Doctrine
The U-2 Incident
USS *Nautilus*

SCIENCE

Rachel Carson
Julius Robert Oppenheimer
Hyman George Rickover
Albert Sabin

Jonas Salk
Sound Barrier
Space Flight

ARTS AND LETTERS

Abstract Expressionism
William Faulkner
Robert Frost

Edward R. Murrow
Carl Sandburg

LABOR

A.F.L.-C.I.O.
John Llewellyn Lewis
George Meany

Walter Reuther
Taft-Hartley Act

POLITICAL DEVELOPMENTS

G.I. Bill of Rights
The Peace Corps

The Twenty-Second Amendment

FOREIGN AFFAIRS

The Holocaust

The Korean War

A

ABSTRACT EXPRESSIONISM.
Perhaps the most distinctively
American art movement in history,
Abstract Expressionism dominated
the art scene in the United States
from the late 1940s to the early
1960s. The "New York School,"
leaders of the Abstract Expressionism movement centered in New
York City, included many veterans
of the Depression-era arts commis-
sions and federal arts projects initiated by President Franklin D.
Roosevelt (1882–1945). Strongly
influenced by European surrealist
and abstract artists—such as Joan
Miro (1893–1983), Fernand Leger
(1881–1955), Piet Mondrian (1872–
1934), and Max Ernst (1891–
1976)—who fled to America during
World War II, the American artists
who pioneered Abstract Expressionism sought a new artistic format that
would allow them to express time-
less, universal emotional content
through an individual, highly personal artistic act. Dissatisfied with
the traditional social realism, and
also with the geometric abstractions
of more contemporary artists, the
New York School developed a non-
representational, vivid, and emo-
tionally charged art form that
emphasized the use of both color
and mass. The most famous artist of
the New York School, Jackson Pollock (1912–1956), in 1946 began his
trademark "drip paintings," produced by spreading enormous can-
vases across the floor and splattering
them with paint thrown from brushes
or poured directly from one-gallon
cans. Other Abstract Expressionists
include Willem de Kooning (born
1904), Mark Rothko (1903–1970),
Barnett Newman (1905–1970),
Robert Motherwell (born 1915),
and Arshile Gorky (1904–1948).
Each artist developed a dramatic,
uniquely personal style, but all val-
ued the expressive qualities of paint
and other artistic materials and
the bold use of colors more highly
than the painted image itself. For
the Abstract Expressionists, who
stressed the spontaneous, impulsive,
emotional application of paint, the
act of painting itself became the
ultimate artistic expression. The
struggle of the artist with his or her
materials expressed the more universal process of self-creation, self-
definition, and the creation of human
values.

A.F.L.-C.I.O. The 1955 merger of
the American Federation of Labor
(A.F.L.) and the Congress of
Industrial Organizations (C.I.O.)
made the new A.F.L.-C.I.O. the
largest and most powerful labor organization in the United States. The
A.F.L.-C.I.O. concentrated on political action and lobbying activities
for pro-labor legislation, leaving the
task of collective bargaining to its
individual member unions. The
A.F.L. was founded in 1886 by
skilled workers who demanded—
and won—shorter hours, higher
wages, and improved working conditions. The C.I.O., founded in
1935 by **John L. Lewis** (*see*), who
led the organization until 1940, was
originally proposed as a division of
the A.F.L., but the A.F.L., limiting
its membership to skilled trade and
craft unions, quickly expelled the
ten unions involved in the C.I.O.
The C.I.O., organizing semi-skilled
and unskilled workers employed in
factories and other mass-production
industries, advocated social reforms
that would better the labor and living
conditions of the American working
class in the midst of the Great Depression. The two organizations had
already collaborated on the foundation of the International Confedera-
tion of Free Trade Unions, designed
to strengthen unions in non-
Communist nations, and had overcome similar internal dissention
—the A.F.L. banishing Communist
unions in 1949 and 1950 and the
C.I.O. expelling the International
Longshoremen's Association for
corruption in 1953. In 1952, when
George Meany (*see*) became head
of the A.F.L. and **Walter Reuther**
(*see*) became president of the
C.I.O., the two new leaders tenta-
tively explored the idea of a merger,
spurred on by Meany's offer of equal
partnership to the C.I.O. The two
organizations officially merged on
December 5, 1955, forming the
A.F.L.-C.I.O. Although in the early
years, the A.F.L.-C.I.O. struggled
with internal tensions, including the
expulsion of the vast Teamsters'
Union in 1957, it rose to become a
powerful political force during
Meany's 24-year reign as president.
Under Lane Kirkland (born 1922),
who succeeded Meany as president
in 1979, the A.F.L.-C.I.O. cur-
rently represents over 100 unions
and has over 17,000,000 members,
a figure representing 18% of the
total U.S. labor force and 78% of all
unionized workers.

ACHESON, Dean Gooderham
(1893–1971). As Secretary of State
(1949–1953) under President **Harry
S. Truman** (*see*), Acheson helped
develop and implement a policy of
containment to prevent Communist

Dean Acheson

expansion by extending American economic and military aid to foreign nations such as Greece and Turkey. Born in Connecticut, Acheson graduated from Yale University in 1915. After interrupting his studies to serve as an ensign in the Navy during World War I, he received his law degree from Harvard University in 1918 and spent the next two years as private secretary to Supreme Court Justice Louis D. Brandeis (1856–1941). From 1921 to 1933, Acheson practiced law in Washington, D.C. In 1933, President Franklin D. Roosevelt ('1882–1945) appointed him Undersecretary of the Treasury, but he resigned the following November because he opposed the President's plan to raise prices by devaluating the international gold rate. Returning to his law practice, Acheson also headed a committee to study the federal government's administrative bureaus in 1939–40. In 1940, he became an active member of the Committee to Defend America by Aiding the Allies, an organization that opposed a negotiated peace with Germany and advocated full-scale aid to Britain. These activities led to Acheson's appointment as Assistant Secretary of State in 1941, a position he held until 1945. He was instrumental in the passage of the Lend-Lease Act, subsequently helped to administer the aid program, and played a significant role in planning the United Nations. As Undersecretary of State from 1945 to 1947, Acheson chaired a committee to plan for the international control of atomic energy. With the intensification of the cold war with the Soviet Union after 1946, Acheson shifted from a conciliatory position and became an ardent champion of containment. Acheson resigned in June, 1947, but returned as Truman's Secretary of State in January, 1949. In Europe, he was active in implementing the Marshall Plan and establishing **NATO** (*see*). In Asian affairs, Acheson attempted to dissociate the United States from the Nationalist Chinese regime on Formosa

(Taiwan), a policy severely criticized in Congress. He was also attacked for the administration's policy regarding Korea. In defining the American "defensive perimeter" in the Far East in January, 1950, Acheson excluded both Formosa and Korea from the areas that the United States agreed to defend. That June, the North Korean Communists attacked South Korea, touching off the **Korean War** (*see*). After his resignation from the State Department in 1953, he returned to his law practice and later served as a spokesman and foreign policy consultant to Democratic Presidents **John F. Kennedy** and **Lyndon B. Johnson** (*see both*). He wrote many books and articles on politics and diplomacy, including *Present at the Creation: My Years in the State Department* (1969), which won the Pulitzer Prize for History in 1970.

B

BAY OF PIGS INVASION. The first major international crisis faced by President **John F. Kennedy** (*see*) occurred on April 17, 1961, when approximately 1,000 Cuban exiles, supported by American aircraft, invaded their homeland at the *Bahia de Cochinos* (Bay of Pigs) in an attempt to overthrow the government of Premier Fidel Castro (born 1927). The Cuban refugees had been trained by the U.S. Central Intelligence Agency (C.I.A.) during the administration of President **Dwight D. Eisenhower** (*see*). The C.I.A., underestimating Castro's strength, had persuaded Kennedy that a large number of Cubans were eager to unseat Castro, and that the project would succeed without deeply involving the United States. Within three days of the landing most of the invaders had been captured, resulting in lost prestige for the United States, which had appeared powerless in the face of a small and supposedly weak adversary. The C.I.A. fell under censure for med-

dling in the internal affairs of another country, and for initiating, rather than carrying out, foreign policy.

BERLIN AIRLIFT. From June, 1948, until May, 1949, the Allies airlifted supplies to Berlin in order to prevent the starvation of 2,500,000 Berliners or a Russian takeover of the entire city. Like all Germany, Berlin had been divided into zones of occupation following the Nazi defeat in World War II, but the city, about 100 miles from the nearest Allied border, lay entirely within the Russian-controlled sector. In the last week of June, 1948, Soviet Premier Joseph Stalin (1879–1953) ordered a blockade, halting all land and water transportation between Berlin and the western zones of occupied Germany. Faced with the alternative of abandoning Berlin or fighting to preserve its status, General Lucius D. Clay (born 1897), the U.S. military governor, sent for General Curtis LeMay (born 1906), commander of the air forces in Europe, to determine the possibility of flying in supplies for the American garrison. Acting on LeMay's advice, President **Harry S. Truman** (*see*) gave the order for the airlift to proceed. Initially, C-47 cargo planes, capable of carrying three tons of foodstuffs and medical supplies each, were used to supply the garrison. It soon became apparent that the Allies would have to feed the entire city of 2,500,000 people. By mid-July, 1,500 tons a day were being flown in by the Americans and 500 tons a day by the British. The planes took off from Frankfurt and Wiesbaden and landed at Tempelhof airfield in the American sector, Gatow airfield in the British sector, and, after November, Tegel airfield in the French sector. As the weather grew colder and more supplies of coal became necessary, the volume increased to 7,000 tons a day. By December, 300 C-54s, capable of carrying 10 tons each, were available for use. Night and day, despite bad weather, the weariness of pilots, and accidents (61 airmen were killed during the 11 months), the deliveries continued. On Easter Sunday, 1949, a record total of 1,398 flights were made (one plane landing every 62 seconds), and 12,941 tons were delivered. A month later, on May 12, 1949, the crisis ended when the Russian government finally abandoned its blockade of Berlin. The airlift, however, was continued for three more months in case the blockade was resumed. In all, 2,300,000 tons of food supplies had been flown into the city on 276,926 flights. However, the split between East and West Germany had become more permanent. A democratic West German government, the Federal Republic of Germany, was established on September 21, 1949. A month later, the Russians established the German Democratic Republic, in East Germany.

BETHUNE, Mary McLeod (1875–1955). A well-known black educator who founded Bethune-Cookman College in Daytona Beach, Florida, Bethune was a special adviser on minority affairs to President Franklin D. Roosevelt (1882–1945) and directed the Division of Negro Affairs in the National Youth Administration from 1936 to 1944. In addition, she served as a consultant on interracial affairs at the first conference of the United Nations in San Francisco. Born in South Carolina, Bethune graduated from Moody Bible Institute in Chicago and began a career in education in 1897, teaching at schools in Georgia and Florida until 1903. In 1904, she established the all-black Daytona Normal and Industrial School for Girls, persuading wealthy businessmen to contribute funds and selling fried fish and sweet-potato pies door to door to raise capital. Bethune served as president of the school, which later became Bethune-Cookman College until 1942. Bethune founded the National Council of Negro Women, was an important figure

Mary McLeod Bethune

UPI

in the National Association for the Advancement of Colored People (N.A.A.C.P.), and served as vice-president of the Commission on Interracial Cooperation of the National Urban League. A close friend of Eleanor Roosevelt (1884–1962), she also presented President **Harry S. Truman** (*see*) at a Liberian presidential inauguration. During World War II, Bethune assisted the Secretary of War in choosing the first Officers Candidate Schools for the Women's Auxiliary Army Corps (W.A.A.C.). She received numerous awards and honorary degrees for her contributions to interracial harmony in the United States.

BROWN VS. BOARD OF EDUCATION of Topeka, Kansas. *See* **School Desegregation; Warren, Earl.**

BUNCHE, Ralph Johnson (1904–1971). The grandson of a slave, Bunche became a diplomat of world renown and a winner of the Nobel Peace Prize for efforts to restore peace in the Middle East. Born in Michigan, Bunche graduated from

the University of California in 1927. Receiving a master's degree in government from Harvard the following year, he became an instructor of political science, and later chairman of the department, at Howard University in Washington, D.C. In 1932, Bunche returned to Harvard for a doctorate in government. After furthering his studies in anthropology and colonial policy at universities in the United States, London, and Capetown, South Africa, on a 1936–37 post-doctoral fellowship, Bunche became a researcher at the Carnegie Corporation, where he helped prepare *The American Dilemma* (1944), a noted study of blacks in America. After America's entry into World War II in 1941, Bunche joined the staff of the Office of Strategic Services (O.S.S.) as a senior social-science analyst. One year later, he became its chief research analyst on Africa and the Far East. In 1944, Bunche entered the State Department as an expert on Africa and dependent areas, helping draft sections on non-self-governing territories and trusteeships that were later written into the charter of the United Nations. In 1945, Bunche was appointed associate chief of the Division of Dependent Area Affairs, the first black to become an acting division chief in the history of the State Department. In 1947, Bunche became director of the Trusteeship Division of the U.N. Secretariat, the New York *Herald Tribune* calling him "as well qualified as is humanly possible for the post." In December of that year, Bunche was named chief secretary to the U.N. Palestine Commission. Following the assassination of Count Folke Bernadotte (1895–1948), the U.N. mediator in the Palestine dispute, Bunche was named acting mediator. He successfully negotiated the Israeli-Egyptian armistice in 1949. This diplomacy earned him the Nobel Peace Prize in 1950, the first black to be so honored. In 1957, Bunche was appointed U.N. Undersecretary for Special Political affairs, the highest position ever held by an American in the Secretariat. He supervised the U.N. emergency force organized to mediate the Suez crisis in 1956 and four years later actively helped settle the Congo crisis. He retired in 1971 because of ill health.

C

CARSON, Rachel Louise (1907-1964). The publication of this biologist's *Silent Spring* in 1963 alerted the world to the dangers of indiscriminate pesticide use, leading to major pesticide-control legislation and a new movement to preserve the ecological balance of the world. Carson, born in Springdale, Pennsylvania, graduated from the Pennsylvania College of Women, where she had set aside her ambition to become a writer in order to study biology, in 1929. While enrolled in a master's program at Johns Hopkins University, she joined the faculty of the University of Maryland in 1931. Five years later, Carson began working as an aquatic biologist and writing radio scripts for the United States Bureau of Fisheries. When the bureau later became the U.S. Fish and Wildlife Service, Carson served as the service's editor-in-chief until 1952. Her first book, *Under the Sea Wind* (1941), won praise for its peaceful prose as well as its scientific accuracy. Carson's second book, *The Sea Around Us* (1951), a national bestseller for over a year, won the National Book Award and has since been translated into 32 languages. *Silent Spring*, her final bestseller, sparked the greatest controversy. In 1963, the President's Science Advisory Committee confirmed Carson's assertions that unregulated pesticide use endangered the world's natural ecological balance. Although she died before seeing the passage of the pesticide-control legislation she had prompted, in 1980 Carson was posthumously awarded the Presidential Medal of Freedom, the nation's

Rachel Carson

highest civilian honor, for her life-long commitment to ecological and environmental protection and for her vision of the interrelatedness of all life.

CASTRO (Ruz), Fidel (born 1926). As the leader of the Cuban revolution, Fidel Castro presided over the development of the first Communist nation in the Western hemisphere. This development sparked fear and distrust in the United States, still gripped by the anti-Communist fervor of the 1950s. Born in Cuba and educated as a lawyer at the University of Havana, Castro was seeking election to the Cuban Parliament in 1952, when General Fulgencio Batista (1901–1973) overthrew the government and established himself as dictator. Castro organized a democratic alliance of rebels that, though small, gradually won enough support among Cuban citizens to force Batista from power in 1958. The United States officially recognized the government set up by Castro and his followers in 1959, but broke off political and trade relations in 1961 after Castro seized privately held land—including property owned by the United States—and entered into trade agreements with the Soviet Union. Despite U.S. objections, Cuba has continued to depend on economic aid from the U.S.S.R. ever since. In April, 1961, the U.S. instigated the **Bay of Pigs Inva-**

sion (*see*), a covert attack on Cuba by a group of Cuban exiles. Castro's defeat of the invaders embarrassed the United States government and helped solidify Castro's political standing in Cuba. Declaring Cuba a "Socialist" nation that year, he announced his committment to a "Marxist-Leninist" program adapted to Cuba's needs. In October, 1962, aerial photographs led the United States to suspect that the Soviet Union had begun installing nuclear missile bases in Cuba. The "Cuban Missile Crisis," which raised worldwide concern because it involved the two largest nuclear powers, subsided only when the Soviet Union agreed to remove the missiles. Although Castro has occasionally asserted political opinions independent of the Soviet party line, he supported Marxists in Africa by sending Soviet-armed Cuban troops to fight for the Communists in Angola and Ethiopia during the 1970s. Since coming to power, Castro has improved Cuba's health services, working conditions, housing, and educational system.

CIVIL-RIGHTS MOVEMENT. The Supreme Court decision in the case of *Brown v. Board of Education of Topeka, Kansas,* ruling unanimously that segregation in public schools was unconstitutional, did more than spur the desegregation of schools. It sparked the conscience of a nation, and awakened blacks in the United States to the possibility that they might finally win, in all aspects of community life, the "equal protection of the laws" guaranteed by the Fourteenth Amendment. In many communities of the South, blacks were still deprived of the right to vote, to use the same facilities of the whites, to eat in the same restaurants, and to work in many factories. In the North, blacks often found themselves discriminated against in jobs and crowded into slums because of unwritten restrictions barring them from white neighborhoods, imposing a sort of de facto segregation. The Court's ruling opened up a new vision of equality for all Americans, regardless of race or color, but the struggle—as yet unfinished—to realize that dream would involve years of suffering, violence, and bitterness. On December 1, 1955, Rosa Parks (born 1913), a black seamstress, refused to give up her seat on a Montgomery, Alabama, bus or to move to the back of the bus. Her arrest sparked a yearlong bus boycott by Southern blacks that ultimately led to a December, 1956, Supreme Court decision that declared all segregation ordinances unconstitutional. The Reverend Dr. Martin Luther King, Jr. (1929–1969), whose lifelong advocacy of non-violence and achieving change through passive resistance—boycotts, sit-ins, marches, and picketing—would earn him the Nobel Peace Prize, gained national recognition through the bus boycott. The boycott also contributed to the Civil Rights Act of 1957, the first civil-rights legislation enacted since the Reconstruction era following the Civil War (1861–1865). However, progress was slow because the act was largely unenforceable (black voters in the South, for example, had increased only 3% by 1960), and the nation's blacks continued to demand immediate action. In February, 1969, black students in Greensboro, North Carolina, led a sit-in protesting segregated lunch counters, and other communities quickly followed their lead. The ineffectiveness of the Civil Rights Act of 1960, like its predecessor aimed primarily at voter registration, prompted further action by Southern blacks. In May, 1961, the Congress of Racial Equality (C.O.R.E.) sponsored integrated "freedom rides" throughout the South to protest discrimination on interstate buses and in public bus depots. Both whites and blacks participating in the freedom rides became targets of violence. The frustratingly slow progress toward racial equality split black activists

into two factions. Like Dr. King, the National Association for the Advancement of Colored People (N.A.A.C.P., founded in 1910), led by its counsel **Thurgood Marshall** (*see*), fought to achieve racial equality through legal means—through legislation and court orders. But in the early 1960s, more and more blacks joined the Black Muslim movement, which advocated black self-defense, separatism, and racial superiority. The rise in power of the Black Muslims (founded in 1934), was led by Malcolm X (1925–

Poster, made by children in Wisconsin, manifests the new racial pride.

1965), who attacked the institutionalization of American racism. In April and May, 1963, televised coverage of Birmingham, Alabama, marches that demanded an end to racial discrimination in employment and public facilities brought the violence of racism home to the American public. Millions saw Birmingham police break up the peaceful demonstrations by attacking the protesters with fire hoses, dogs, and clubs—even using them against children. By the end of that summer, similar protests, rallying behind the song "We shall overcome," had crowded over 15,000 demonstrators into Southern jails. On August 28, 1963, Dr. King led a March on Washington, where over 250,000 blacks and whites gathered around the Lincoln Memorial to demand immediate action. Most observers credit this demonstration with providing the show of force needed to pass the Civil Rights Act of 1964, the first comprehensive legislation abolishing discrimination in public accommodations and employment. The act differed significantly from the earlier civil-rights bills in denying federal funds to discriminatory public institutions, and in authorizing the Attorney General to enforce the act. The Civil Rights Act of 1964 remains the most comprehensive civil-rights legislation ever enacted in the United States. Yet the blacks were still denied the right to vote in many restrictive sections of the South, and, recognizing that enfranchisement held the key to political power, voting rights became the next goal of the civil-rights movement. (*Entry continues in Volume 17.*)

D

DEWEY, Thomas Edmund (1902-1971). Despite widespread predictions that he would win the 1948 Presidential election, this well-known "racket-buster" and former Republican governor of New York

Thomas E. Dewey

cases. Dewey continued his racket-busting activities as district attorney of New York County from 1937 to 1941, and in 1942 he was elected to the first of three successive terms (1943–1955) as governor. Dewey achieved a record of efficiency, economy, and political moderation in state administration. As a result, he received the Republican Presidential nomination in 1944. He lost the election to Franklin D. Roosevelt (1882–1945) by 432 electoral votes to 99 but polled more than 22,000,000 popular votes—the largest number cast for a Republican in 16 years. In his 1948 campaign, Dewey campaigned on the theme: "It's time for a change." His defeat confounded political analysts as well as the Chicago *Daily Tribune*, which ran a front-page headline "DEWEY DEFEATS TRUMAN" even before all the polls had closed on election day. Dewey's poor showing in the supposedly secure Republican states of the Middle West contributed to yet another Democratic victory, with Truman gaining a margin of more than 2,000,000 popular votes and winning 303 electoral votes to Dewey's 189. Dewey, reentering state politics, became leader of the Eastern wing of the Republican Party, and helped engineer the party's nomination of General **Dwight D. Eisenhower** (*see*) in 1952. In 1955, Dewey retired from the governor's office and returned to his law practice, remaining an elder statesman of his party.

DIRKSEN, Everett McKinley (1896–1969). One of the few great orators to serve in Congress in recent times—always quick to spice his remarks with Biblical allusions—Dirksen was a Representative for 16 years before his election in 1950 to the Senate where he served until his death. The most influential Republican in Congress after he became the party's Senate leader in 1959, he became noted for several foreign and domestic policy reversals. Born

lost in a stunning political upset to his Democratic opponent, **Harry S. Truman** (*see*). A native of Owosso, Michigan, Dewey graduated from the University of Michigan in 1923 and received a law degree from Columbia University two years later. He practiced law in New York City until 1931, when he was appointed chief assistant to the U.S. attorney for the Southern District of New York. In 1935, Dewey became a special prosecutor, investigating organized crime in New York, and soon earned a nationwide reputation for his successful drives against narcotics, the vice traffic, and the notorious group of contract killers, Murder Incorporated. He obtained convictions in all but one of 73

in Pekin, Illinois, Dirksen served with the Army in France during World War I and subsequently held several minor offices in Illinois before entering Congress in 1933. In Washington, Dirksen attended night school and received his law degree in 1936. Rapid about-faces for ideological reasons or political expediency quickly became a Dirksen trademark. For example, he voted against many New Deal measures advocated by President Franklin D. Roosevelt (1882–1945) but supported two of them: the Social Security Act (1935) and the Minimum Wage Act (1938). In foreign policy, Dirksen at first was an isolationist. However, a few months before the Japanese attacked Pearl Harbor on December 7, 1941, he reversed his stand and urged all Republicans to show "a unity of purpose" by backing Roosevelt's foreign policy. In 1954, Dirksen steadfastly supported Senator **Joseph R. McCarthy's** (*see*) increasingly unpopular anti-Communist "witchhunt." Dirksen subsequently became famous for three major policy reversals. In 1962, he abandoned his opposition to **John F. Kennedy's** (*see*) request

Everett M. Dirksen

for authority to buy United Nations bonds in order to make up deficits largely resulting from French and Soviet refusals to make peace-keeping payments to the U.N. "I will not charge my conscience with any act or deed which would contribute to the foundering of the United Nations," he declared. The following year, Dirksen initially opposed the ratification of the **nuclear test-ban treaty** (*see*), but later voted for it. In March, 1964, Dirksen attacked the Civil Rights Act, mainly because he opposed granting the power to enforce nondiscrimination in public housing and jobs to the federal government. However, two months later, he supported the bill, commandeering enough Republican votes—27 out of 33—to secure its passage.

DOUGLAS, William Orville (1898–1980). Considered the most liberal member of the Supreme Court for 35 years—the longest term in U.S. history—Douglas frequently dissented in defending the civil liberties guaranteed by the First Amendment to the Constitution. After graduating from Columbia Law School in 1925, Douglas worked for a Wall Street law firm and, in 1928, joined the faculty of Yale Law School. There he became a specialist in business law, which led to his appointment to the Securities and Exchange Commission (S.E.C.) in 1934 by Joseph P. Kennedy (1888–1969), whom Douglas succeeded as chairman of the S.E.C. in 1936. An advocate of the New Deal, he pursued a policy of reform on the S.E.C., investigating bankrupt businesses and reorganizing the nation's stock exchanges. In 1939, President Franklin D. Roosevelt (1882–1945) named Douglas, a close friend, to the Supreme Court. At 40, the youngest Justice to be named to the Court in 125 years, Douglas soon earned a reputation for liberal views, brilliance, and a colorful character. Roosevelt considered Douglas as a

running mate in the 1944 elections but chose **Harry S. Truman** (*see*) who became president when Roosevelt died the next year. Years later, Douglas maintained that had he been Roosevelt's vice-president, "there would have been no Hiroshima" and the Cold War with the Soviet Union might have been avoided. On the bench, Douglas's legal opinions have expressed his belief that "The American government is premised on the theory that if the mind of man is to be free, his ideas, his beliefs, his ideology, his philosophy must be placed beyond the reach of government." During the so-called McCarthy era (*see* **Joseph McCarthy**) in the early 1950s, Douglas and Justice Hugo Black (1886–1971) disagreed with the Court and constantly maintained that even Communists had the right to free speech. In 1953, Douglas tried to stay the execution of convicted spies, Julius and Ethel Rosenberg (*see* **Rosenberg spy case**). As a result, an unsuccessful attempt was made by conservatives in the House of Representatives to impeach him. A second effort was made to impeach Douglas because of his "moral character" after he married his fourth wife in 1966. Although the Supreme Court became increasingly conservative during his years on the bench, Douglas remained a voice of liberalism, refusing to let popularity dictate his decisions. Douglas retired from the Supreme Court in 1975.

DULLES, John Foster (1888–1959). As Secretary of State from 1953 to 1959 under President **Dwight D. Eisenhower** (*see*), Dulles dominated the formulation and execution of American foreign policy. A militant anti-Communist, he considered neutralism immoral, advocated the "liberation" of Communist-held areas of Eastern Europe, and believed that the threat of massive nuclear retaliation would prevent Communist aggression. These policies, coupled with his de-

termination to go "to the brink" of nuclear war, if necessary, made him an extremely controversial world figure. Dulles was accused of "brinkmanship" after promising the peoples of Soviet-dominated Eastern Europe in January, 1953, that they could "count on us." However, the following June, when East German workers rioted, and in 1956, during the Hungarian uprising against the Soviet Union, he took no steps to help "liberate" either people. Born into a wealthy, Washington, D.C., family, Dulles spent much of his youth with his grandfather, John Watson Foster (1836–1917), who was Secretary of State in 1892 under President Benjamin Harrison (1833–1901). Dulles graduated from Princeton University in 1908 and subsequently studied law at George Washington University Law School before he was admitted to the New York bar in 1911. During World War I, he served on the War Industries Board, and in 1919 was legal counsel to the American delegation to the reparations committee at the Paris Peace Conference. Dulles then returned to the practice of law, serving as a financial consultant to several foreign governments. In the late 1930s, he began a long political association with the Republican politician, **Thomas E. Dewey** (*see*), and when Dewey won the party's presidential nomination in 1944, Dulles became his adviser on foreign policy. The following year, he became senior United States adviser at the San Francisco conference that drafted the charter of the United Nations. He occasionally served as a delegate to the U.N. General Assembly from 1946 to 1950. In July, 1949, Dewey, then governor of New York, appointed Dulles to complete the Senate term of Robert F. Wagner, Sr. (1877–1953), who had resigned, but Dulles lost the seat in a special election held the following November. In 1950, President **Harry S. Truman** (*see*) named him ambassador-at-large, and as such, he was the chief author and negotiator of the Japanese Peace Treaty of 1951. As Secretary of State under Eisenhower, Dulles enjoyed an unprecedented degree of authority because of the President's confidence in him and America's prestige as a major world power. He traveled extensively, flying more than 500,000 miles on missions throughout the world. Dulles created a network of local treaties—his critics accused him of "pactomania"—designed to align the United States with as many non-Communist nations as possible, even those with Fascist governments. The two most important international organizations that Dulles helped forge were the Central Treaty Organization (CENTO) in the Middle East and the **Southeast Asia Treaty Organization** (*see*), both established in 1954. In the Far East, Dulles and Eisenhower refused to help the French in Vietnam in 1954. They also declined in 1954–55 to provide military support to help Nationalist China defend the offshore islands of Quemoy and Matsu against the Communist Chinese, although Dulles pledged the United States to protect Taiwan. In the Middle East, he adopted a supportive stand toward Britain, France, Israel, and other allies, and played a critical role in developing the so-called Eisenhower Doctrine of January, 1957. The President announced that the United States would give economic aid and was "prepared to use armed force" in the Middle East in the event of "aggression from any country controlled by international Communism."

This doctrine was invoked in May, 1958, when the United States sent marines into Lebanon after pro-Egyptian elements, allegedly under Communist influence, threatened its government. Due to ill health, Dulles resigned his position in April, 1959, and died of abdominal cancer a month later. Dulles published *War, Peace, and Change* (1939) and *War or Peace* (1950).

E

EISENHOWER, Dwight David (*Continued from Volume 15*). A national hero following his achievements as Supreme Commander of Allied forces in Western Europe during World War II, Eisenhower was courted by the Democrats, who wanted him to run as their Presidential candidate in 1948. The General refused and, instead, accepted the presidency of Columbia University. He also served as a military adviser in Washington, D.C., and as Supreme Commander of the armed forces of the **North Atlantic Treaty Organization** (*see*) from 1950 to 1952. In 1952, Eisenhower waged a close campaign against Senator Robert A. Taft (1889–1953) and won the Republican Presidential nomination. In what was essentially a personality contest with his Democratic opponent, **Adlai E. Stevenson** (*see*), Eisenhower pledged to "clean up the mess in Washington," balance the budget, and end the Korean War. That November, he polled about 34,000,000 popular votes, almost 7,000,000 more than Stevenson, and won 442 electoral votes to Stevenson's 89. Eisenhower's election as the 34th President of the United States returned the Republicans to power for the first time in 20 years. Eisenhower believed in pri-

A 1952 Eisenhower campaign button.

vate enterprise, less federal involvement in local government, and espoused a policy of "moderate Republicanism" in domestic affairs. During his administrations, he helped establish the Department of Health, Education, and Welfare and the federal Interstate Highway System, expand Social Security benefits, increase minimum wages, introduce urban renewal, and develop water resources. Price and wage controls imposed during the Korean War were eliminated, foreign aid was scaled down, and, in order to balance the budget and cut taxes, the federal payroll was reduced. Using the same methods he employed as the head of Allied forces in Europe, Eisenhower delegated much of his responsibilities to his Secretary of State, **John Foster Dulles** (*see*), his Vice-President Richard M. Nixon (born 1913), and other cabinet and White House advisers. Eisenhower traveled to Korea in December, 1952 and, with Dulles, negotiated a truce in the Korean War in July, 1953. An internationalist, Eisenhower also committed himself to the security of West Germany and tried to improve relationships with nations in the Middle East, Far East, and Latin America. He presented an "Atoms for Peace" proposal to the United Nations in 1953, and in 1954 helped found the **Southeast Asia Treaty Organization** (*see*). In 1955, he attended the Geneva Summit Conference with British Prime Minister Anthony Eden (1897–1977), French Premier Edgar Faure (born 1908), and Soviet leaders Nikita Khrushchev (1894–1971) and Nikolai Bulganin (1895–1975). The reunification of Germany, European security, disarmament, and cultural and trade exchanges were discussed. Although no agreements were reached, the meeting closed on a note of optimism, and Eisenhower's statements gave the world renewed hope for peace. During 1953 and 1954, Eisenhower was faced with a growing controversy over Senator **Joseph R. McCarthy** (*see*) of Wisconsin. The President chided McCarthy for his Communist "witch-hunt" tactics but did nothing to curb his activities. Then, in September, 1955, Eisenhower suffered a heart attack—the first of several major illnesses that he was to have while in office. He nevertheless decided to run for a second term in 1956. Campaigning on his record of peace and prosperity—which was enhanced by his insistence on a cease-fire and the withdrawal of French and British troops from the Suez Canal in October, 1956—Eisenhower again defeated Stevenson, receiving 35,600,000 votes to Stevenson's 26,000,000 and 384 more electoral votes than Stevenson. In January, 1957, the President changed his stand on the Middle East, announcing the "Eisenhower Doctrine," which pledged America's use of force if necessary to protect the area from Communist aggression. After 1955, Eisenhower had to contend with a Democratic control of Congress, and with momentous problems at home and abroad. In September, 1957, he dispatched federal troops to Little Rock, Arkansas, to enforce a federal court order desegregating a local high school, an action that antagonized Southerners while it was applauded in the North. In October, 1957, the Soviet Union orbited its first unmanned satellite, Sputnik I (*see* **Space Flight**), thus causing doubts throughout the world about American technical superiority. Business slumped sharply in the winter of 1957–58 and only slowly recovered. In the summer of 1958, Sherman Adams (1899–1986), a Presidential assistant and one of Eisenhower's closest friends, was accused of peddling influence in federal agencies on behalf of his friends and was forced to resign. With Eisenhower's prestige at a low during the Congressional elections of November, 1958, the Democrats won control of Congress by the wid-

est margin since 1936 and subsequently thwarted some of the President's programs. In September, 1959, Eisenhower's talks with Soviet Premier Khrushchev during the latter's visit to the United States, produced a temporary thaw in the cold war. However, the **U-2 Incident** (*see*) in May, 1960, ended the detente and caused the collapse of a scheduled summit conference. Although Eisenhower had hoped to improve ties with Latin-American nations, he was forced to break off diplomatic relations with Cuba in January, 1961 after **Fidel Castro** (*see*) had confiscated U.S. landholdings and business concerns and had demanded a drastic cut in the personnel of the American Embassy in Havana. Eisenhower supported Vice-President Nixon in his unsuccessful campaign for the Presidency in 1960. After **John F. Kennedy** (*see*) entered the office in January, 1961, Eisenhower retired to his farm in Gettysburg, Pennsylvania. He died of heart failure on March 28, 1969, a month after undergoing ab-

dominal surgery, and was buried in Abilene, Kansas.

F

FAULKNER, William Cuthbert (1897–1962). Considered one of the world's greatest modern writers, William Faulkner wrote stories, set in the American South, that were distinguished by long, insightful narratives involving profound commentary on the human condition. He grew up in Oxford, Mississippi, where his father ran a livery stable and was business manager of the University of Mississippi. Faulkner left high school before graduating, but he read widely and, by his late teens, had begun to write poetry and short stories. After Faulkner left high school, he was an air force cadet, a bank clerk, a bookstore clerk, a postmaster, and scoutmaster. He also attended college briefly, then moved on to New Orleans, where he wrote sketches for a local newspaper. With the encour-

William Faulkner

agement of author Sherwood Anderson (1876–1941), Faulkner wrote his first novel, *Soldier's Pay* (1926). His second novel, *Mosquitoes* (1927), was a mildly satirical novel about literary life in New Orleans. Faulkner's third novel, *Sartoris* (1929), was rejected by one publisher and published by another only after he shortened it. Faulkner wrote *Sartoris*, the first in a series of related novels and stories about the mythical Yoknapatawpha County, based on the people and history of his native Mississippi. In 1929, Faulkner published his fourth novel, *The Sound and the Fury*, but because he still could not earn enough money through writing alone, he took a job shoveling coal at night in a local power plant. During that night-shift, he wrote his next novel, *As I Lay Dying* (1930), which critics have called a "tour de force." Over the next two decades, Faulkner produced some of his finest works, including *Light in August* (1932), *Absalom, Absalom!* (1936), and *Go Down, Moses* (1942), in which his famous story, "The Bear," appeared. Faulkner developed a his own distinctive version of the "stream-of-consciousness" style, in which he would narrate a train of thought, often shifting abruptly from one point of time to another. While some critics objected to the intense demands such writing placed on the reader's attention, others noted that Faulkner's vivid descriptions of human affairs resulted in stories of great "emotional power." Due to continuing financial difficulties, he worked in Hollywood periodically, writing such movie scripts as *To Have and Have Not* (1944), an adaptation of an Ernest Hemingway (1899–1961) novel, and *The Big Sleep* (1946), both of which starred Humphrey Bogart (1899–1957) and Lauren Bacall (born 1924). The completion of *The Portable Faulkner* (1946), an anthology prepared by Malcom Cowley (born 1918), brought popular attention to Faulkner's work. In 1950, Faulkner was awarded the Nobel Prize for Literature. Both *Collected Stories* (1950) and *A Fable*, a novel published in 1954 to mixed reviews, received the National Book Award for Fiction, and *A Fable* won the Pulitzer Prize as well. As Faulkner became a well-known figure, he publicly opposed segregation during the racial disputes in the 1950s. He published more fiction, including *The Town* (1957), *The Mansion* (1959), and *The Reivers* (1962). From 1958 until his death in 1962, he lived in Oxford and Charlottesville, Virginia, where he lectured at the University of Virginia. Faulkner drank excessively throughout his adult life, often requiring the aid of his family and friends to recuperate from heavy binges. In 1962, Faulkner entered a hospital after one of his drinking bouts; he died there of a heart attack on July 7. Much of Faulkner's fiction depicts tragedy and violence, as well as racial, sexual, and generational conflict. However, in his Nobel acceptance speech, he asserted a positive view, declaring: "I believe that man will not merely endure; he will prevail. He is immortal, . . . because he has a soul, a spirit capable of compassion and sacrifice and endurance."

FORRESTAL, James Vincent (1892–1949). A firm believer in the importance of building and maintaining the military power of the United States, Forrestal expanded the U.S. Navy to meet the demands of World War II, and became the first Secretary of Defense. Born in Beacon, New York, Forrestal was educated at Dartmouth and Princeton, but he lacked the money to finish college and, in 1916, went to work as a bond salesman for an investment bank in New York City. He served in the Navy overseas during World War I. After the war, Forrestal returned to the bank, later known as Dillon, Read and Company, becoming its president in 1937. In 1940, a year before the United States entered World War II, President Franklin D. Roosevelt (1882–1945) appointed Forrestal Under-Secretary of the Navy. Forrestal, promoted to Secretary of the Navy in 1944, directed the expansion of the Navy from a small, peacetime force to the more than 1,000 combat ships and 50,000 auxiliary vessels with which the United States fought the war. In 1946, after the war had ended, Forrestal strongly opposed President **Harry S. Truman's** (*see*) plan to merge the Army and Navy together into one department, arguing that such a department would be so large that its civilian head would be unable to control it effectively. He helped devise an alternative scheme, enacted by Congress in 1947, creating the new position of Secretary of Defense. As a member of the President's Cabinet, the Defense Secretary would advise the President on military policies and programs and have authority over the Secretaries heading each military branch—Army, Navy, and Air Force. Truman appointed Forrestal, esteemed for his effective leadership, as the first Secretary of Defense. In the continuing debate over the extent to which the United States should expand its military power in view of the rise of Communism abroad, Forrestal argued that—even in peacetime—the President should seek a large annual military budget from Congress, to build U.S. power. Forrestal also proposed a permanent civil service corps and universal military training as an alternative to selective service. Truman, disagreeing with him over the amount of the military budget, ultimately chose to request less from Congress than Forrestal's more ambitious proposals. Despite his enormous influence, by the end of 1948, Forrestal was severely disappointed that he had not won more support for his views. Seriously depressed, Forrestal was admitted to a hospital for psychiatric care. He committed suicide in May, 1949.

FROST, Robert Lee (1874–1963). One of the nation's greatest poets and the recipient of four Pulitzer Prizes, Frost wrote about the character, people, and life of New England, finding universal significance in all his subjects. Born in San Francisco, Frost moved to New England when he was 10 years old and lived there most of his life. He studied briefly at Dartmouth College and at Harvard University and worked as a bobbin boy in a Massachusetts cotton mill. He also worked as a shoe maker, a newspaper editor, a schoolteacher, and a farmer. His main ambition, however, was to be a poet, and he went to England in 1912 because he believed the British were more appreciative of poets. During his three years there, he published his first two volumes—both about New England—*A Boy's Will* (1913) and *North of Boston* (1914). *North of Boston* contains many of his most famous poems, including "Mending Wall," "Home Burial," and "The Death of a Hired Man." Upon returning to America in 1915, Frost settled on a New Hampshire farm. The following year, he published *Mountain Interval*, a collection that included "Birches" and "The Road Not Taken." The latter contains the lines that indicated the direction of his own life:

> *Two roads diverged in a*
> *wood, and I—*
> *I took the road less traveled by,*
> *And that made all the differ-*
> *ence.*

In 1924, Frost was awarded the first of his four Pulitzer Prizes for *New Hampshire* (1923), a volume of poems that included, "Stopping by Woods on a Snowy Evening" and "Fire and Ice." His other Pulitzer prize-winning collections were *Collected Poems* (1930), honored in 1931; *A Further Range* (1936), the winner in 1937; and *A Witness Tree* (1942), which won in 1943. Frost also taught and lectured at several colleges and universities, including Amherst College and Michigan and Harvard universities. In tribute to his lifework, Frost was asked to read a poem at the inauguration of President **John F. Kennedy** (*see*) on January 20, 1961. He wrote one especially for the occasion but stumbled over the lines and instead then recited his "The Gift Outright." When the gentle, white-haired poet died two years later at the age of 89, Kennedy said, "Frost leaves a vacancy in the American spirit."

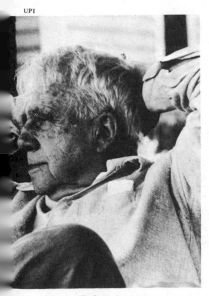

Robert Frost

G

G.I. BILL OF RIGHTS. This Congressional action, officially known as the Serviceman's Readjustment Act of 1944, supported the post-war economy and improved the educational level throughout the nation by providing special educational and economic assistance to United States veterans returning home from World War II combat. Any honorably discharged veteran who had served at least 90 days during the war was eligible to receive the benefits instituted under the G.I. Bill. These benefits included up to $500 per year for four years of educational or vocational training, expenses for books and fees, and federally funded living allowances of $50 per month for single veterans and $75 per month for veterans with dependents. The bill provided for special job placement benefits through the U.S. Employment Service, up to 52 weeks of unemployment insurance ($20 per week), and loans of up to $2,000 (increased to $4,000 in 1945) guaranteed by the Veterans Administration, for the purchase of a house, farm, or the establishment of a business. During the next decade, some 7,800,000 veterans took advantage of the educational benefits, the most popular program established under the bill. In all, over 13,000,000 veterans took advantage of the educational provisions of the G.I. Bill, including veterans of the **Korean War** (*see*) and the Vietnam War, covered by later extensions of the Act, making access to higher education in the United States more democratic for three generations of veterans. It also prevented the U.S. labor market from becoming glutted with over 10,000,000 returning veterans. And the G.I. Bill's housing provisions, dramatically increasing the demand for better housing throughout the United States, sparked an unprecedented suburban building boom that changed the face of the nation.

H

HISS, Alger (born 1904). A high-ranking official in the State Department from 1936 to 1947, Hiss was the central figure in a sensational case of alleged espionage by agents of Communist Russia. Born in Baltimore, he was an outstanding student at Johns Hopkins University, before graduating in 1926. After obtaining a degree from the Harvard Law School in 1929, he served as secretary to Supreme Court Justice Oliver Wendell Holmes, Jr. (1841–1935). Hiss practiced law in Boston and New York from 1930 to 1933 and then moved to Washington, working for the Agricultural Adjust-

Alger Hiss

ment Administration (1933–1935) and the Department of Justice (1935–36) before joining the State Department in 1936. Considered one of the most capable of young New Deal officials, he accompanied Franklin D. Roosevelt (1882–1945) to several important international meetings, including the Yalta Conference in 1945. Hiss served as secretary general at the charter meeting of the United Nations in San Francisco. Hiss resigned from government service in 1947 to assume the presidency of the Carnegie Endowment for International Peace. The following year, Whittaker Chambers (1901–1961), a magazine editor who claimed he had known Hiss in the 1930s when both were members of the Communist Party, told the House Committee on Un-American Activities that Hiss had stolen and handed over to him secret government documents. Representative **Richard M. Nixon** (*see*) of California was instrumental in investigating Chambers' allegations, all of which

were denied by Hiss. Accused of lying under oath, Hiss was indicted in 1948 and brought to trial the following summer. The evidence against Hiss was controversial, and Chambers was described as a "psychopathic personality" and a chronic liar. Nevertheless, after a first jury failed to reach a verdict, the second jury found Hiss guilty on two counts of perjury in January, 1950. Hiss was imprisoned until November, 1954. Three years later, he published *In the Court of Public Opinion*, in which he maintained his innocence. Hiss later entered business and engaged in lecturing and teaching in the New York area.

THE HOLLYWOOD TEN. In October, 1947, ten movie directors, screenwriters, and producers called before the House Committee on Un-American Activities, refused to confirm or deny allegations that they were Communists. Although they invoked the protection of the Fifth Amendment, which guarantees the right to refuse to provide testimony against oneself, their sentences ushered in a decade of Hollywood "blacklisting." The Hollywood Ten included screenwriter Ring Lardner, Jr. (born 1915), an Academy Award (Ocsar) winner (for *Woman of the*

Year in 1946) who would later earn another Oscar for his *M*A*S*H* screenplay. Another member of the group was Dalton Trumbo (1905–1976), who won an Oscar in 1956 for best screenplay (*The Brave One*). He wrote under the pseudonym Robert Rick, but was unable to claim his award due to the blacklist. The others who refused to testify before the committee were screenwriters Alvan Bessie (born 1904), Lester Cole (born 1904), Albert Maltz (1908–1985), Samuel Ornitz (1890-1957), and John Howard Lawson (1894–1977), one of the founders and the first president of the Screen Writers' Guild; producer Adrian Scott (1912–1972); and directors Herbert J. Biberman (1900–1971) and Edward Dmytryk (born 1904). Except for Dmytryk, who eventually admitted his Communist sympathies and served only two months in jail, each received a one-year sentence and a fine. The imprisonment of the Hollywood Ten and the anti-Communist fervor of the fifties, spurred on by the theatrics of Senator **Joseph R. McCarthy** (*see*), gave rise to Hollywood's blacklisting policy, which denied work to anyone even accused of radical sympathies. Many other careers, including those of actors John Garfield

The Hollywood Ten: l. to r., Robert Adrian Scott, Edward Dmytryk, Samuel Ornitz, Lester Cole, Herbert Biberman, Albert Maltz, Alvan Bessie, John Howard Lawson, Ring Lardner, Jr. Not shown, Dalton Trumbo.

(1913–1952) and Larry Parks (1914–1975), were ruined by rumors of Communist leanings. The blacklisting policy would not end until 1959, when those formerly barred from consideration for Oscars were readmitted into the nominating process. On May 2, 1975, Dalton Trumbo finally received the Oscar he had earned almost twenty years earlier under a pseudonym.

HOLOCAUST. Although as early as May, 1942, the Allies knew of the Holocaust—Nazi Germany's methodical persecution, imprisonment, enslavement, torture, and murder of 6,000,000 European Jews from 1933 to 1945—the liberation of German concentration camps at the war's end still horrified the world. Upon rising to power, Adolf Hitler (1889–1845) immediately began to legislate his anti-Semitism in an attempt to rid Germany of all Jews. The first concentration camps—at Dachau, Oranienburg, and Buchenwald—opened in 1933, Hitler's first year as Chancellor. Later, the Nuremberg Laws (1935) instituted Nazi boycotts of Jewish businesses, limited Jewish access to schools and professions, and prohibited marriage or sexual intercourse between Jews and non-Jews. Prewar persecution of the Jews culminated in *Kristallnacht* ("the night of broken glass") on November 9–10, 1938, when Nazi storm troopers burned 267 synagogues, arrested almost 30,000 Jews, and later fined German Jews $400,000,000 for the damage inflicted on their property. Although Germany made no effort to conceal its policy—or its ultimate objective—no other nation took any effective action to rescue or shield the Jews. After the onset of World War II, the Nazis expanded their plan of extermination to include all European Jews. Under German occupation, Polish Jews were crowded into ghettos, employed as slave labor in the Nazi war economy, and dragged to death camps—Germany's "final solution to the Jewish

question," made official policy at the Wannsee Conference of German leaders in January, 1942. On September 29–30, 1941, as many as 30,000 Jews were machine-gunned at the Babi Yar Ravine in Kiev, Ukraine. Jewish resistance to this terrorism, unaided by the Allied powers, almost invariably brought still more destruction: In the Warsaw Uprising (April–May, 1943), 60,000 Polish Jews who had protested the imprisonment of 450,000 of the city's other Jews were captured or killed themselves. In the Nazi death camps, Jewish prisoners, herded into the camps on freight cars, were subjected to medical experimentation (in accordance with Hitler's fanatic desire to establish a "master race"), regarded as slave labor, slowly starved to death, or quickly murdered with cyanide gas, carbon monoxide, electrocution, flamethrowers, machine guns, or hand grenades. At the end of the war, the evacuation of Auschwitz, where over 2,000,000 Jews had been murdered, left an indelible impression on all those who saw it— whether in person, on film, or in photographs. The appalling sight of

thousands of naked, emaciated, crippled Jewish survivors staggering through the prison gates, leaving behind the piles upon piles of rotting corpses will never be forgotten. These images shook the faith of many in both God and civilization, and prompted a question that, over 40 years later, still has never been adequately answered: "Why?"

HOOVER, John Edgar (1895–1972). The man who built the Federal Bureau of Investigation into one of the world's most effective law enforcement agencies, Hoover headed the FBI for almost 50 years, reappointed without regard to political party by eight Presidents. A native of Washington, D.C., Hoover worked as a messenger at the Library of Congress while attending night classes at George Washington University, from which he received his law degree in 1916. The following year, he went to work for the Department of Justice. After World War I, he became a special assistant to Attorney General A. Mitchell Palmer (1872–1936), organizing a series of raids that resulted in the arrest and deportation of hundreds of

J. Edgar Hoover

alleged Communists and radical organizers. The operation was severely criticized as a flagrant violation of the Constitution's guarantee of due process. In 1921, Hoover became deputy director of the Justice Department's 13-year old Bureau of Investigation. After the Teapot Dome Scandal in 1923 exposed widespread corruption in the Bureau, Attorney General Harlan Fiske Stone (1872–1946) Hoover was made the Bureau's director. Hoover fired corrupt officials within the agency, eliminated political influence in appointments, and instituted a merit system for promotions. An innovative organizer, Hoover developed a central fingerprint file, a scientific crime library, and a training academy for state and local police. He established high standards for FBI agents, recruiting only lawyers and accountants, and maintained a high, almost tyrannical level of discipline. His agents had no union or tenure and could be transferred around the country at Hoover's direction. Initially, the Bureau's activities were restricted to uncovering bank frauds and pursuing violators of the prostitution-curbing Mann Act. During Hoover's directorship, the FBI's criminal jurisdiction expanded continuously. The so-called Lindbergh Law in 1932 designated kidnapping as a

federal offense, and Hoover's FBI solved an incredible 99% of such crimes. Bank robbery also became a federal crime after it was discovered that bank robbers could evade capture by local police by crossing state lines. During the 1930s, FBI agents shot it out with such highly publicized bank robbers as John Dillinger (1904?–1934), Charles "Pretty Boy" Floyd (1907?–1934), and Arizona "Ma" Barker (?–1935). As World War II approached, the FBI turned its attention to national security. Within 72 hours of the Japanese attack on Pearl Harbor on December 7, 1941, the FBI had taken into custody 3,846 enemy aliens and seized large quantities of contraband arms. During the war, the FBI captured German saboteurs who had landed on Long Island and in Florida. The bureau continued its spy-chasing activities into the 1950s, this time in pursuit of Communists. Amid the furor created by the anti-Communist investigations of Senator **Joseph R. McCarthy** (*see*), critics wondered if the FBI would not return to the high-handed practices of A. Mitchel Palmer. "The FBI," Hoover replied, "will always strive to preserve the civil liberties of every American citizen. We can never become . . . a Gestapo." In 1956, Congress passed a law making it a federal crime to travel across

state lines in order to violate gambling, extortion, or bribery laws, putting organized crime under the jurisdiction of the FBI. Prodded by President Lyndon B. Johnson (1909–1973), Hoover reluctantly marshalled the FBI to enforce civil rights laws in the 1960s. Finding local police in the South uncooperative, the FBI established a network of informers within the racist Klu Klux Klan. In 1964, President Lyndon B. Johnson waived the mandatory retirement requirement on Hoover's 70th birthday, and he was reappointed to his post when President Richard M. Nixon (born 1913) took office in 1969. Hoover's last years as director saw a storm of controversy regarding the invasion of privacy involved in the FBI's monitoring of the personal lives of student activists, radicals, and civil rights leaders such as Martin Luther King, Jr. Hoover, a lifelong bachelor, died in office in 1972.

K

KEFAUVER, Carey Estes (1903–1963). A liberal Democrat, Estes Kefauver earned national prominence as the chairman of a Senate investigation into organized crime, as a candidate for the 1952 Democratic Presidential nomination, and

Senator Estes Kefauver swears in a witness before the Senate Crime Investigation Committee.

The Kennedy family posed a few days after John was elected President. Seated, left to right, are his sister Mrs. R. Sargent Shriver, his parents Mr. and Mrs. Joseph Kennedy, his wife Jacqueline, and brother Edward. Standing are Mrs. Robert F. Kennedy, brother-in-law Stephen Smith, Mrs. Smith, the President-elect, Robert Kennedy, sister Mrs. Peter Lawford, brother-in-law R. Sargent Shriver, Mrs. Edward Kennedy, and brother-in-law Peter Lawford.

as **Adlai E. Stevenson's** (*see*) running mate in the 1956 campaign for President. Born on a Tennessee farm, Kefauver graduated from the University of Tennessee and from Yale University Law School, practiced law in Tennessee, and in 1939 won election to the U.S. House of Representatives. Kefauver served in that office for the next ten years, and was elected to the U.S. Senate in 1948. Known as liberal but independent, he supported civil rights legislation and favored curtailment of monopolies. By 1951, he had gained recognition as the chairman of the Senate Crime Investigation Committee, whose televised hearings exposed organized crime to the nation. In 1952, Kefauver sought the Democratic nomination for President but lost to Adlai Stevenson, who was defeated in the general election by **Dwight D. Eisenhower** (*see*). In

1958, Kefauver won the nomination as the Democratic candidate for Vice-President defeating Senator **John F. Kennedy** (*see*) on the third ballot at the Democratic convention. He and Stevenson campaigned unsuccessfully against the incumbent Republican candidates, Eisenhower and Richard M. Nixon (born 1913). Continuing to serve as a U.S. Senator until his death in 1963, Kefauver conducted investigations into illegal monopolies and price-fixing, and successfully sponsored the Drug Safety Act, which Congress passed in 1962.

KENNEDY, John Fitzgerald (1917–1963). The 35th President of the United States and the first Roman Catholic to be Chief Executive, Kennedy—who was only 43 when elected—brought a youthful exuberance and a new emphasis on the arts

to the White House. He had passed crucial tests in foreign relations and was attempting to implement a far-reaching domestic program when he was assassinated on November 22, 1963. Kennedy was born in Brookline, Massachusetts, the second son of financier and diplomat, Joseph P. Kennedy (1888–1969). In 1938, he worked as a secretary for his father, then ambassador to Great Britain. Kennedy drew on his European experience in writing his undergraduate thesis, later published as *Why England Slept* (1940). He graduated cum laude from Harvard in 1940, became an ensign in the Naval Reserve in October, 1941, and was assigned in April, 1943, to the South Pacific. On August 2, Kennedy's torpedo boat, the *PT-109*, was rammed and sunk by a Japanese destroyer. Kennedy ordered his men to swim the three miles to shore, and he himself towed a wounded crew member, receiving several medals for bravery. Four months later, he returned to a hospital near his home to recuperate from malaria and to receive treatment for the back injury he received in the sinking. There, he learned that his older brother, Joseph P. Kennedy, Jr. (1915–1944), had been killed while on an air mission over the English Channel. After the war, John worked briefly as a journalist before running as a Democrat in Massachusetts for the House of Representatives. With help from his family and Navy friends, Kennedy won convincingly and was twice reelected (1947–1953). As a Representative, he generally supported the domestic programs of President **Harry S. Truman** (*see*) but was occasionally critical of foreign policy, particularly with regard to the Far East. In April, 1952, Kennedy announced he would run for the Senate, opposing incumbent Henry Cabot Lodge, Jr. (1902–1985). Though the Republican Presidential candidate, **Dwight D. Eisenhower** (*see*) carried Massachusetts by more than 200,000 votes, Kennedy defeated Lodge by 70,000 votes. While recuperating from two back operations, he wrote the Pulitzer Prize-winning *Profiles in Courage* (1956), portraits of political leaders who defied public opinion to take a stand on what they believed was right. Kennedy bid for the Democratic Vice-Presidential nomination in 1956 after the party's Presidential candidate, **Adlai E. Stevenson** (*see*), threw the nomination open to the convention. However, he lost on the third ballot to **Estes Kefauver** (*see*) of Tennessee. After winning reelection to the Senate in 1958, Kennedy decided to seek the Presidency in January, 1960. He won the Democratic primary in New Hampshire easily, but the key tests were in Wisconsin, where Hubert H. Humphrey (1911-1978) was popular, and West Virginia, where Kennedy's religion and wealth were considered drawbacks.

In capturing 56% of the vote in Wisconsin and 61% in West Virginia, Kennedy insured a first-ballot nomination. His chief rival, Lyndon B. Johnson (1908–1973), was chosen as his running mate to give balance to the ticket. In his acceptance speech, Kennedy pledged to explore a "New Frontier" encompassing "uncharted areas of science and space, unsolved problems of peace and war, unconquered pockets of ignorance and prejudice, unanswered questions of poverty and surplus." The turning point of the campaign was a series of four televised debates between Kennedy and the Republican nominee Richard M. Nixon (born 1913). Kennedy appeared handsome, relaxed and confident, while Nixon appeared haggard and uncertain. Kennedy won the election by a narrow margin—just a little over 100,000 votes out of nearly 69,000,000 cast, and received 303 electoral votes to Nixon's 219. At Kennedy's inauguration, he declared, "Ask not what your country can do for you—ask what you can do for your country." Kennedy gathered a group of brilliant, young aides to assist him in carrying out his programs. He named his brother Robert F. Kennedy (1925–1968) Attorney General; Pierre Salinger (born 1925), press secretary; R. Sargent Shriver, Jr. (born 1915), a brother-in-law, head of the newly created Peace Corps; Theodore C. Sorensen (born 1928), a major speech writer; and Arthur M. Schlesinger, Jr. (born 1917), a historian, his special assistant. Kennedy was initially occupied with a series of international crises. The **Bay of Pigs Invasion** (*see*) of Cuba in April, 1961, which had been planned by the Eisenhower administration, resulted in a fiasco. Next, a Communist take-over threatened Laos. Kennedy considered intervention but settled for a guarantee of Laotian neutrality. However, he slowly increased military aid to South Vietnam, stationing about 16,000 American troops and mili-

tary advisers there. In June, 1961, Kennedy met with Russian Premier Nikita Khrushchev (1894–1971) in Vienna, but they were unable to reach any agreements. In August, the East Germans built the Berlin Wall, sealing off West Berlin. Two years later, Kennedy underscored American support of West Germany, declaring in a speech in Berlin, "*Ich bin ein Berliner* (I am a Berliner)." Earlier in October, 1962, Kennedy faced the gravest crisis of the cold war when he learned that Russia was installing offensive missiles in Cuba. Kennedy ruled out both an air strike and passive acceptance of the Russian challenge, imposing instead a naval quarantine of the island, with a pledge that the United States would not invade Cuba if the Russians halted further missile delivery and dismantled the ones that were there. The following year, a **nuclear test ban treaty** (*see*) was negotiated with Russia and more than 100 other nations. A two-way "hot line" was installed in the summer of 1963 to provide instant communications between the White House and the Kremlin in Moscow. In addition, Kennedy established the Peace Corps, which sent young Americans to help underdeveloped nations throughout the world, and the Alliance for Progress, to aid Latin America. His most persistent domestic problem was civil rights (*see* **Civil-Rights Movement**). Although he waited 22 months to sign an executive order ending racial discrimination in federal housing, he sent federal marshals to enforce integration at the University of Mississippi. Kennedy endorsed the March on Washington in August, 1963, a peaceful rights demonstration led by Martin Luther King, Jr. (1929–1968) and pressed for the passage of the most comprehensive civil-rights bill in the nation's history. However, the bill and most of Kennedy's other domestic legislation were stalled in Congress at the time of his death. In preparation for seeking reelection in

Dr. Martin Luther King, Jr., receives the Nobel Peace Prize in 1964.

1964, Kennedy decided to visit Texas to try to unite the warring Democratic factions there. On November 22, 1963, while riding in an open limousine through downtown Dallas with his wife, Jacqueline (born 1929), and the governor of Texas, John B. Connally (born 1917), and his wife, Kennedy was shot by Lee Harvey Oswald (1939–1963), a left-wing political extremist. Vice-President Johnson, who had been riding in the third car behind Kennedy's in the motorcade, was sworn in as President two hours later aboard Air Force One at Dallas's Love Field. Kennedy was buried on November 25 in Arlington National Cemetery after a funeral attended by many world leaders and watched by millions of mourners on television. The day before the funeral, Oswald was shot by Dallas nightclub owner Jack Ruby (1911–1967) while being transferred to another jail. Ruby was arrested, tried, convicted, and sentenced to death. The conviction was reversed by a Texas court of appeals. Ruby died of cancer in January, 1967, while awaiting a retrial. After Kennedy's assassination, rumors spread that Oswald might have had accomplices or that a conspiracy was involved. A special commission, headed by

Chief Justice **Earl Warren** (*see*), concluded after taking testimony from 552 witnesses that Oswald had acted alone, but the conspiracy rumors were never fully laid to rest.

KOREAN WAR. This prolonged and bloody struggle resulted in over 2,000,000 casualties. The first major war of the nuclear age pitted the newly founded Republic of Korea (ROK, or South Korea), backed by troops from sixteen members of the United Nations (U.N.), against North Korea, supported by Communist China and the Soviet Union. In 1945, the Japanese surrender in World War II had left Korea divided at the 38th parallel, with Soviet troops occupying the north and American troops controlling the south. After the Soviet Union ignored a call by the United Nations for free elections throughout Korea in May, 1948, the U.N. officially recognized the Republic of Korea as the only true Korean government on August 15, 1948. By June, 1950, the ROK Army, comprised of 100,000 troops and 500 U.S. military advisers, still had little weaponry and were poorly organized; the 130,000 troops in North Korea, by contrast, had received full training and modern weaponry from the

U.S.S.R. The Korean War began on June 25, 1950, when, in a surprise dawn attack, North Korean troops crossed the 38th parallel and pushed toward Seoul, the South Korean capital. Both the United Nations and the United States responded immediately: The U.N. Security Council called for immediate withdrawal of North Korean troops that same day, and two days later President **Harry S. Truman** (*see*) ordered U.S. air and sea cover for ROK troops. On June 30, two days after North Korea had captured Seoul, Truman ordered ground support as well; the next day, American troops at Osan engaged in their first fight with North Koreans. On July 7, authorized by a U.N. resolution calling for a unified command of its troops, Truman appointed General Douglas MacArthur (1880–1964) commander of all U.N. forces. The advancing North Korean Army had overrun almost all of South Korea by September 15, 1950, when American troops led by MacArthur executed a daring amphibious landing in Inchon Harbor, well within territory then occupied by North Korean troops. The surprise move split the North Korean Army in two, isolating those troops north of the city, and enabled the U.S. troops to recapture Seoul on September 26 and take over 125,000 North Korean prisoners. By October 1, ROK troops had pushed the North Korean Army back beyond the 38th parallel and continued to advance, seizing Pyongyang—the North Korean capital—on October 19, and capturing almost all of Korea by October 26, when they reached the Yalu River—the border between Korea and the Chinese province of Manchuria. Communist China now entered the war on the side of North Korea, surprising MacArthur, who had insisted the Chinese would enter the war only if U.S. troops advanced into Manchuria. On November 25–26, when 180,000 Chinese troops pushed across the Yalu River, forcing MacArthur's U.N. troops to retreat. On December 31, 1950, over

400,000 Chinese and 100,000 North Korean troops—opposed by just 100,000 Americans, 100,000 South Koreans, and a small number of troops from 13 other U.N. members—crossed the 38th parallel again, recapturing Seoul on January 4, 1951. Under the leadership of field general Matthew B. Ridgway (born 1895), the U.N. forces began counteroffensive attacks on January 25, retaking Seoul on March 14–15 and reestablishing the front line at the 38th parallel on March 31. On April 11, President Truman stunned the American public and the U.N. allies by relieving MacArthur of duty and replacing him with General Ridgway. MacArthur had challenged Truman's authority, loudly criticizing the President's hesitancy to bomb, blockade, and even invade China, a reluctance supported by U.S. allies in Europe, who wanted to avoid the risk of bringing the Soviet Union into the war and a possible nuclear confrontation. On July 10, the first truce talks were held at Kaesong on the 38th parallel. They would continue on and off for the next two years. By November, the negotiations had moved to Panmunjom and Ridgway had ordered his troops to discontinue offensive operations, reducing the role of U.N. forces to actively defending the front line. On April 28, 1952, Communist negotiators insisted that all prisoners taken by U.N. forces— even those who expressed no desire to return—be repatriated in their native lands. In May, General Mark W. Clark (1896–1984) replaced Ridgway, who accepted a post at the command headquarters of the **North Atlantic Treaty Organization** (*see*), as U.N. commander. On October 8, 1952, the truce talks broke off and the war continued in a bloody stalemate, damaging to both sides, with the Communist ground strength (800,000 troops against 300,000 U.N. and ROK troops) offset by the U.N. air superiority. On March 28, 1953, the Communists accepted a U.N. proposal to exchange 6,670

sick and wounded prisoners for 684 ailing prisoners (including 149 Americans) held by the Communists. After this breakthrough, truce talks resumed on April 26. In June, Syngman Rhee (1875–1965), president of the Republic of Korea, announced his intention to refuse any armistice that failed to reunite Korea. Although close to reaching an agreement, the Communists, accusing the U.N. delegation of "bad faith," withdrew from the truce talks, initiating the final battles of the war. Despite this setback, the two sides signed an armistice agreement on July 27, 1953. (Although Rhee kept his word and refused to sign, he observed the terms of the agreement.) At the war's end, the Communists had suffered an estimated 1,600,000 casualties (almost 1,000,000 of them Chinese) and 580,000 U.N. and ROK troops (including 160,000 Americans) had been killed, wounded, or captured. The war had cost the United States $67,000,000,000 and 54,000 American lives (34,000 in combat and 20,000 through injuries or disease). In September, 1953, an exchange of 88,559 prisoners took place, but 14,227 Chinese, 7,582 North Koreans, 325 South Koreans, 21 Americans, and one Briton refused to return to their native lands. Although the Republic of Korea had gained approximately 1,500 square miles of territory, the end of this costly war left Korea still divided according to the final front line: roughly the 38th parallel, the same point at which the war began.

L

LEWIS, John Llewellyn 1880–1969). Rising from the depths of the coal mines to become one of the most powerful labor leaders in the twentieth century, Lewis led the United Mine Workers (U.M.W.) union for forty years. The son of a coal-mining Welsh immigrant father who had himself been a union activ-

ist, Lewis left school after seventh grade and became a miner at the age of fifteen. He quickly climbed up the union ranks, heading the U.M.W. locals in Lucas, Iowa and Panama, Illinois, lobbying for the union in Illinois, and becoming general field agent of the U.M.W.'s parent organization, the American Federation of Labor (A.F.L.) in 1911. In 1920, Lewis won election as president of the U.M.W., and fifteen years later he gained a national reputation by organizing the Committee for Industrial Organization within the A.F.L. However, in its devotion to trade and craft unions, the A.F.L. refused to acknowledge the need for industrial unions and tried to dismantle to C.I.O. When ten prominent C.I.O. unions, including the U.M.W., ignored an order to disband, the A.F.L. expelled them all (*see* **A.F.L.-C.I.O.**). As the first president of the reorganized and newly independent Congress of Industrial Organizations (C.I.O.), Lewis introduced orchestrated effective strikes in the previously unorganized automobile and steel industries, among others. After resigning as president of the C.I.O. in 1940, Lewis pulled the U.M.W. out of the C.I.O. in 1942 and led miners' strikes during World War II that won higher wages for its members but lost the support of a public feeling the pressure of a wartime economy. The new hostility to unions that helped produce the **Taft-Hartley Act** (*see*) led Lewis to seek greater strength for the U.M.W. by rejoining the A.F.L. in 1946, but he withdrew again a year later. In 1946, he suffered his greatest defeat when President **Harry S. Truman** (*see*) ordered the federal government to seize all bituminous coal mines, quickly ending a coal miners' strike Lewis had initiated. In both 1947 and 1948, Lewis ignored federal court injunctions that prohibited his union from striking and was subsequently convicted of contempt of court; both he and the U.M.W. were fined. In 1952, after an Illinois mining accident that

John L. Lewis

killed 119 men, Lewis persuaded Congress to set federal safety standards for mines. After retiring in 1960, Lewis chaired the board of trustees of the U.M.W.'s welfare and retirement fund until his death.

M

McCARTHY, Joseph Raymond (1909–1957). This Republican Senator from Wisconsin gave his name to the practice of making unsubstantiated accusations of disloyalty and using unfair methods of investigations: McCarthyism. The center of bitter controversy during the early 1950s after he charged that several government agencies and the army harbored Communists, "Communist-sympathizers," and spies, he was censured by the Senate for numerous abuses. McCarthy, born on a farm near Appleton, Wisconsin, studied law at Marquette University in Milwaukee. Admitted to the Wis-

consin bar in 1935, McCarthy was soon involved in local politics, first as a Democrat and then as a Republican. In 1939, he was elected to a circuit-court judgeship in Wisconsin. Commissioned a lieutenant in the Marine Corps in 1942, he served as an intelligence officer in the Pacific Theater. While still on active duty, he returned to Wisconsin in 1944 to campaign—in uniform—for the Republican Senate nomination but was defeated in the primary election. In 1948, he won the Republican nomination for the Senate over the former Progressive Party member, Robert M. La Follette, Jr. (1895–1953). McCarthy then easily defeated his Democratic opponent in November. He immediately initiated a controversy with **John L. Lewis** (*see*) president of the United Mine Workers Union, by suggesting that striking miners be drafted into the Army. In February, 1950, McCarthy charged that there were 205 "known Communists" in the State Department, then headed by **Dean Acheson** (*see*). This was the first of five McCarthy investigations now widely regarded as a "witch hunt" that cost many citizens their reputations and their jobs. McCarthy was soon called before a special subcommittee of the Senate Foreign Relations Committee and asked to substantiate

his charges. After extensive testimony, during which McCarthy was unable to identify a single Communist in the State Department, the committee, headed by Maryland Senator Millard E. Tydings (1890–1961), accused him of perpetrating "a fraud and a hoax" and termed his accusations "irresponsible" and "untruthful." Later in 1950, an investigation by the Senate Committee on Privileges and Elections found that McCarthy and his supporters had helped to engineer Tydings's reelection defeat in a "despicable 'back street' type of campaign." Undeterred, McCarthy launched an attack on the Democratic administrations of President Franklin D. Roosevelt (1882–1945) and **Harry S. Truman** (*see*), terming them "twenty years of treason." McCarthy antagonized **Dwight D. Eisenhower**, then the head of the military forces of the **North Atlantic Treaty Organization** (*see both*), when he questioned the loyalty of Eisenhower's former army superior, General George C. Marshall (1880–1959). In the fall of 1951, a special Senate subcommittee was formed to investigate McCarthy's financial affairs. The Committee questioned a $10,000 check he had received from a company that had won a $37,500,000 contract from a federal

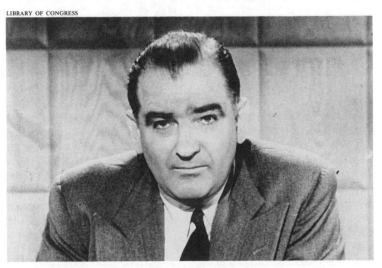

Joseph McCarthy

agency under the jurisdiction of one of McCarthy's committees, but McCarthy refused to testify, contending that the check was for a pamphlet he had written. After winning reelection in 1952, McCarthy returned to the attack, assailing—without result—several of Eisenhower's diplomatic appointees, and soon including the Eisenhower administration in his "treason" charge. In 1953, McCarthy, as chairman of the Permanent Subcommittee on Investigations, began probing alleged "security risks" in the Voice of America and the Army. The nationally televised, 26-day Army-McCarthy hearings occurred in April and May of 1954. McCarthy charged that "subversives" were knowingly employed at various military installations. The Army countered by alleging that McCarthy had tried to secure preferential treatment for a former staff aide, then in service. Several military men were mercilessly cross-examined and subjected to insult by the McCarthy staff. The following December, the Senate voted to "condemn" McCarthy for his contemptuous and abusive conduct. This censure, combined with Democratic control of Congress after the 1954 elections, quickly reduced McCarthy's influence. His health declined rapidly, and three years later he died of acute hepatitis.

MARSHALL PLAN. *See* **Truman Doctrine.**

McNAMARA, Robert Strange (born 1916). As Secretary of Defense in the 1960s, Robert McNamara modernized the United States Defense Department; as president of the World Bank in the 1970s, he expanded international assistance to developing countries; as an independent adviser in the 1980s, he has spoken forcefully on issues of East-West relations. Born in California, McNamara excelled at the University of California at Berkeley and obtained his master's degree at the Harvard University Business School

Robert S. McNamara

in 1939. After World War II, during which he helped coordinate the deployment of U.S. Army troops and planes, McNamara became one of a group of Harvard Business School "Whiz Kids," who went to work for the financially troubled Ford Motor Company. After helping turn Ford back into an efficient, profitable company, McNamara became its president in 1960. In 1961, he left Ford to accept the post of Secretary of Defense under President **John F. Kennedy** (*see*). Centralizing Defense Department control over the government's military branches, McNamara applied his skills of business management and cost-benefit analysis to get more out of the defense budget: By cutting overlapping programs and equipment from the several military branches and coordinating their operations, he forced them to run more efficiently. In 1962, after visiting Vietnam, McNamara became convinced that the U.S. should commit troops and arms to help the South Vietnamese government in its battle against the Communist North Vietnamese. McNamara's support of the 1964 Gulf of Tonkin Resolution,

which enabled the President to send more troops to Southeast Asia, and his support for President Lyndon B. Johnson's (1908–1973) decision to bomb North Vietnam in 1965 made him a target for the many Americans who had started to voice strong opposition to the war. However, by 1967, McNamara no longer supported President Johnson's continued investment in the war; it was costing even more lives and money, with no discernible success. In 1968, McNamara left the government to become president of the International Bank for Reconstruction and Development, also known as the World Bank. Formed in 1945 as an internationally funded source of loans to the world's poorer countries, the World Bank promotes economic development and improved standards of living. Under McNamara, the bank's revenues increased, permitting it to extend further aid to impoverished nations. He steered the bank away from its prior policy of funding large, expensive projects, such as dams and power plants, which benefitted relatively few people, toward a policy of providing developing nations with more broadly needed, inexpensive services such as rural health care, housing and education. Since retiring from the World Bank in 1981, McNamara has spoken and written frequently on the issues of nuclear arms and East-West relations. In particular, he has blamed an unrealistic fear of the Soviet Union and Communism for leading the United States to support repressive foreign governments.

MEANY, (William) George (1894–1980). As the first president of the combined American Federation of Labor and Congress of Industrial Organization (A.F.L.-C.I.O.), Meany concentrated on keeping peace within his mammoth organization rather than on expanding union membership or effecting social or political reforms. The son of an Irish-Catholic plumber who be-

George Meany

came president of a local union, Meany was born and raised in New York City. He became a plumber's apprentice in 1910 and a union member in 1915. In 1922, he was elected business agent for Local 463 of the plumber's union. Within 12 years, the tough spokesman for labor demands rose within union ranks to become president of the New York State Federation of Labor, a 1,000,000-member organization. During the Depression, membership increased and Meany successfully lobbied in New York for pro-labor laws, including an unemployment insurance act. In 1939, Meany won unanimous election as secretary-treasurer of the national A.F.L. In 1941, President Franklin D. Roosevelt (1882–1945) appointed him to the newly formed National Defense Mediation Board. During World War II, Meany served on the War Labor Board and fought against Congressional attempts to make the war effort an excuse for limiting

labor's rights. On becoming president of the A.F.L. in November, 1952, Meany sought to unite the labor movement by merging the A.F.L. with its offshoot, the C.I.O., thus healing a conflict between skilled and unskilled labor that had kept the two organizations divided since 1938. The merger was completed in December, 1955. Meany was elected president of the combined A.F.L.-C.I.O., while **Walter Reuther** (*see*), former president of the C.I.O., became a vice-president in charge of the industrial division. Meany insisted on keeping his organization free of Communist and gangster influences. In December, 1957, the A.F.L.-C.I.O. expelled its largest member, the International Brotherhood of Teamsters, headed by James R. Hoffa (1913–1975?), after investigations led by Robert F. Kennedy (1925–1968) exposed widespread corruption in its ranks.

MURROW, Edward Roscoe (1908–1965). A pioneer of journalism, Murrow became famous for his radio news broadcasts from Europe during World War II, and for his television news programs of the 1950s, which drew attention to important national and world events. Born in North Carolina, Murrow majored in speech and was student body president at Washington State College. In 1935, he joined the CBS broadcasting company, which was then a 100-station radio network. CBS sent him to London in 1937 to direct broadcasts on special cultural and political events. In March, 1938, when Nazi Germany invaded Austria, Murrow flew to the scene and reported the march of Adolf Hitler's (1889–1945) army in Vienna as it was happening. Describing the take-over with dramatic accuracy, Murrow thus established radio as a powerfully direct medium of news. He assembled a team of correspondents to report on the continuing developments in Europe. After World War II began, Murrow himself often broadcast his reports

from the streets of London even during German bomb attacks. Through these broadcasts, which began with his famous opening, "This . . . is London," Murrow described the war to millions of Americans who listened at home. Widely esteemed by the war's end, Murrow joined with a CBS colleague, Fred Friendly (born 1915), to produce a weekly radio news program, "Hear It Now," which later became "See It Now" when it moved to television in 1951. Through this program and various television documentaries— such as "Harvest of Shame," which exposed the plight of poor migrant farm workers—Murrow presented numerous incisive reports on the major issues of his time, including **nuclear testing** (*see*) and the **desegregation of schools** (*see*), and brought major U.S. and world figures under public scrutiny. "See It Now" presented the first television documentary on a U.S. war when Murrow reported on the Korean War during the Christmas of 1952, highlighting the perspective of the Amer-

Edward R. Murrow

ican soldiers fighting in it. With the rise of Communism abroad, Americans began to fear its presence in the United States. During this "Red Scare," members of the broadcasting industry "suspected" of Communist alliance were blacklisted and denied employment (see **Hollywood Ten**). Murrow strongly opposed such repression of civil liberties. In one of the most famous "See It Now" programs, aired in March 1954, he criticized Senator **Joseph McCarthy's** (see) investigative hearings. By publicly displaying McCarthy's assaultive and relentless badgering of witnesses, Murrow exposed McCarthy's fanaticism and contributed to his downfall. During these years, however, television networks began increasingly to emphasize profitable entertainment shows over news programming, and "See It Now" ceased broadcasting in 1958. Condemning this transition, Murrow criticized the television industry for promoting "escapism . . . and insulation from the realities of the world in which we live." He left television, and served as director of the U.S. Information Agency under Presidents **John F. Kennedy** (see) and Lyndon B. Johnson (1908–1973) until lung cancer forced him to retire in 1964.

N

NORTH ATLANTIC TREATY ORGANIZATION. Formed in 1949, the North Atlantic Treaty Organization (NATO) was the first peacetime military alliance in American history. Prompted by the Communist take-over in Czechoslovakia in February, 1948, and the Russian blockade of Berlin (see **Berlin Airlift**) in June of that year, President **Harry S. Truman** (see) determined to take further Soviet advances in Europe. The North Atlantic Treaty was signed in Washington on April 4, 1949, by 12 nations—Belgium, Canada, Denmark, France, Great Britain, Ice-

land, Italy, Luxembourg, the Netherlands, Norway, Portugal, and the United States. Each nation agreed that an armed attack against one nation would be considered an armed attack against all. The U. S. Senate approved the treaty by a vote of 82 to 13 on July 21, 1949. At subsequent conferences, with Secretary of State **Dean Acheson** (see) representing the United States, plans were drafted for the defense of the North Atlantic area and for the creation of a multinational military force. In October, 1949, Congress passed the Mutual Defense Assistance Act, authorizing $1,000,000,000 in military aid to NATO countries. In December, 1950, **Dwight D. Eisenhower** (see) was appointed Supreme Commander of the Allied forces in Europe, with headquarters near Paris. From the start, the military branch of NATO was subject to the civilian control of the North Atlantic Council, which consists of the heads of state, foreign ministers, or ambassadors of the member nations. Greece and Turkey were admitted to NATO in 1952, West Germany became a member in 1955, and Spain joined the alliance in 1982. In the 1960s, heated debates over the continued need for strong conventional forces and over the deployment of nuclear weapons in Europe caused tensions that weakened the alliance. Following the announcement in 1966 by President Charles de Gaulle (1890–1970) of France that nearly all French forces would be withdrawn from NATO, the civilian and military headquarters of NATO were moved to Brussels, Belgium, in April, 1967. In 1974, NATO confronted its greatest challenge: direct military conflict between two of its members. Responding to a Greek-led coup in Cyprus, a small Mediterranean island populated by both Greeks and Turks, Turkey invaded the island in July, 1974. Greece, protesting NATO's refusal to deploy military forces in its behalf, withdrew from the military wing of the alliance. Greece

remained outside NATO's military structure until its reintegration in October, 1980. NATO maintains over 100 army divisions in Europe, some units armed with nuclear weapons, and a strong naval force in the North Atlantic.

NUCLEAR TESTING. The advent of nuclear weapons—which have a destructive power thousands of times greater than conventional bombs and release radioactive particles (fallout) that, carried by the wind, can fall over the entire world—has raised grave fears for the safety of the planet. Although, like any weapon, each newly developed nuclear bomb required testing, the tests—even those conducted under maximum safety conditions—unleashed detectable fallout throughout the world. By the beginning of the 1960s, worldwide concern had prompted international agreements that, while failing to prohibit *all* further testing of nuclear devices, banned testing in the atmosphere, underwater, and in outer space. The United States Army detonated the first atomic bomb, developed under the direction of **J. Robert Oppenheimer** (see), at the remote Alamogordo Air Base in New Mexico on July 16, 1945. The bomb, which had an explosive yield equal to 20,000 tons of TNT, disintegrated the steel tower on which it stood and fused the desert floor beneath it into a radioactive glasslike substance. Less than one month later, President **Harry S. Truman** (see) ordered the first—and only—offensive use of nuclear weapons, dropping two atomic bombs on Japan: one on the city of Hiroshima on August 6, the other on the city of Nagasaki three days later. The first atomic bomb decimated Hiroshima. It destroyed a 47-square-mile area, created fires that gutted the heart of the city, and killed or injured 140,000 of the city's 255,000 residents. Later that year, after the Japanese had surrendered in World War II, Truman introduced legislation that created the first civilian nuclear agency, the Atomic Energy Commission (superseded in 1974 by the Nuclear Regulatory Committee and the Energy Research and Development Agency). By 1949, the Soviet Union had detonated its first atomic bomb, marking the end of the U.S. nuclear weapons monopoly. Beginning in 1950, U.S. scientists began exploring the possibilities of nuclear weapons detonated through nuclear fusion—the joining of radioactive isotopes—rather than fission—splitting the nucleus of an atom. This new grade of weapons, known as thermonuclear bombs or hydrogen bombs, would permit the construction of bombs virtually unlimited in size. Prompted by the unraveling of the **Rosenberg spy case** (*see*), with its disclosure that U.S. nuclear technology had been sent to the Soviet Union, Truman ordered accelerated development of the hydrogen bomb on January 13, 1951. In November, 1952, the U.S. detonated the first thermonuclear device, with the destructive power of several millions of tons of TNT; but less than a year later, Soviet officials announced that they too had tested a hydrogen bomb. The dawning nuclear arms race between the two superpowers—and the acceleration of nuclear weapons testing—raised global questions about the safety of such tests. Because no nuclear weapon is completely free of fallout, atmospheric testing left areas of lingering radioactivity throughout the world. Underwater testing threatened to contaminate the seabed permanently, and underground testing threatened to taint the earth's arable soil, and thus its food supply. In 1958, under the pressure of public opinion, the United States and the Soviet Union agreed to a moratorium on atmospheric testing, but both nations had resumed testing by 1962. That year, the United Nations established the Eighteen-Nation Disarmament Committee (the ENDC, later called the Committee on Disarmament), to work toward international

control and regulation of nuclear weapons. In 1963, the ENDC drafted a test-ban treaty that prohibited atmospheric, underwater, and outer space testing of nuclear devices. Although France and China would not sign the agreement, more than 110 other nations—including both the United States and the Soviet Union—agreed to observe the terms of the treaty, and all testing of nuclear devices was limited to underground detonations.

O

OPPENHEIMER, Julius Robert (1904–1967). Often called the father of the atomic bomb for his work on the development of the first **nuclear weapons** (*see*), Oppenheimer was later labeled a security risk during the "Red Scare" of the 1950s. After graduating from Harvard in 1925, Oppenheimer received his doctorate from Gottingen University in Germany. He joined the faculties of both the University of California and the California Institute of Technology in 1929 and, except for his wartime service (1943–1945), taught there until 1947. Describing his "ivory tower" years, Oppenheimer, a scholar who could converse in eight languages, recalled, "I was almost wholly divorced from the contemporary scene in this country. I never read a newspaper or a current magazine. . . . I had no radio, no telephone; I learned of the stockmarket crash . . . only long after the event." In the midst of World War II, Oppenheimer was put in charge of the main laboratory of the Manhattan Project at Los Alamos, New Mexico, in March, 1943. His staff, eventually over 4,000 scientists and technicians, designed and constructed an atomic bomb. From the time the first bomb was tested in the desert on July 16, 1945, Oppenheimer seemed haunted by its implications, and he repeatedly urged international control of atomic energy. In 1947, he was

UPI

Oppenheimer inspects aftermath of first atomic test in 1945 with the late Maj. Gen. Leslie R. Groves.

named chairman of the general advisory committee to the Atomic Energy Commission (A.E.C.). Despite his objections to the development of an even more powerful hydrogen bomb on moral grounds, President **Harry S. Truman** (*see*) ordered work begun on the first H-bomb. During the 1950s, Oppenheimer became a target of Senator **Joseph R. McCarthy's** (*see*) Communist "witch hunt." Oppenheimer's brother and sister-in-law were both Communist Party workers, and his wife had once been a member. In 1953, President **Dwight D. Eisenhower** (*see*) ordered Oppenheimer's security clearance suspended. A special board of the A.E.C. concluded that Oppenheimer was loyal and discreet but, by a vote of 2 to 1, it recommended the continued suspension of his top-secret clearance. When, on appeal, the entire A.E.C. concurred with the board's recommendation in June, 1954, Oppenheimer returned to the Institute for Advanced Study at Princeton, New Jersey, where he had been director since 1947. He remained officially blacklisted until 1962, when President **John F. Kennedy** (*see*) invited him to the White House. In 1963, for his outstanding contributions to nuclear physics and for laying the foundations for the peaceful uses of atomic energy, Oppenheimer received the A.E.C.'s highest award, named for the nuclear physicist Enrico Fermi (1901–1954). Dr. Oppenheimer's books include *Science and the Common Understanding* (1954), *The Open Mind* (1955), and *Some Reflections on Science and Culture* (1960).

P

PEACE CORPS, THE. Founded in 1961 by President **John F. Kennedy** (*see*), the Peace Corps has promoted mutual meeting and understanding among the United States and other nations by sending over 100,000 volunteers from age 18 to 80 to foreign countries around the world. After proposing the volunteer agency during his 1960 Presidential campaign, Kennedy established the Peace Corps by executive order on March 1, 1961, naming his brother-in-law, R. Sargent Shriver (born 1915), as the temporary agency's first director. The organization became permenent in September, 1961 with the passage of the Peace Corps Act of 1961. The Peace Corps only assigns volunteers to countries that request their presence and only to projects determined by the host country. Volunteers, who must be 18 years old, receive approximately three months of training in the local language, customs, and history, as well as the skills they will need before beginning their two-year term of foreign service. Although the Peace Corps provides only a small monthly expense allowance (about $300) for food, clothing, housing, and incidental expenses, it offers a unique opportunity to work and live in direct contact with the citizens of other nations. The Peace Corps jumped from 900 volunteers in 16 countries in its first year to 12,500 volunteers in 50 nations—primarily in Asia, Africa, and Latin America—in the mid–1960s, at the height of its popularity. Since then, volunteers have dwindled to just under 5,000 a year in over 60 countries. Approximately 35% of today's volunteers work on educational projects; 26% in agricultural or rural development, and 16% in health and nutrition. Although the Peace Corps offers no salary (except for a lump sum totalling $175 per month at the end of one's service), no diplomatic immunity or special privileges, and no exemption from future military service (if required), many find the Peace Corps offers its own rewards. One-third of all volunteers extend their term beyond the original two years of service, and one prominent American—Lillian Carter (1896–1983), mother of President Jimmy Carter (born 1924)—called her two years in the Peace Corps at age 68, "the best thing that ever happened to me."

POWELL, Adam Clayton, Jr. (1908–1972). A civil-rights leader decades before the March on Washington (*see* **Civil-rights Movement**), leader of the nation's largest church congregation, and plaintiff in a landmark Supreme Court case that overturned a House of Representatives vote to bar him from Congress because of allegations of misuse of public funds and several contempt of court citations. Powell served 26 stormy years as the Congressional representative from Harlem, a predominantly black district in New York City. Born in New Haven, Powell grew up in New York, graduated from Colgate University in 1930, and received an M.A. from Columbia in 1932. In 1936, he succeeded his father as pastor of the Abyssinian Baptist Church in Harlem, two years before Shaw University awarded him an honorary doctorate in divinity. His eloquent sermons and his active support of demonstrations aimed at forcing desegregation and winning job opportunities for blacks during the Depression made him a favorite among his congregation, which grew to 14,000 members—the largest in the United States. In 1941, Powell became the first black man to win election to the New York City council. Three years later, he began the first of his many terms in the House of Representatives. From 1960 to 1967, Powell chaired the House Committee on Education and Labor, introducing 48 major pieces of social legislation addressing such problems as poverty, juvenile delinquency, the minimum wage, and vocational training. However, Powell had been sued by a New York City woman whom he had libeled during a 1960 television interview. He had declined to defend himself and lost the suit, becoming liable for over $50,000 in damages, a sum that he refused to pay. After ignoring seven subpoenas to appear before the court to explain his nonpayment, Powell was convicted of criminal contempt of court in November, 1966. Powell immediately took up permanent residence in Bimini, an island in the Bahamas, while continuing to serve in the House. On March 1, 1967, following a Select Committee investigation that advised censuring Powell, the House voted to exclude him from Congress. A special election to fill his seat resulted in another landslide victory for Powell, who won over 87% of the votes cast. After raising money to pay off his debt, Powell returned to Harlem in March, 1968 and won his thirteenth consecutive Congressional election later that year. In

January, 1969, the House voted to seat him in Congress, but fined him $25,000 for alleged misuse of funds and stripped him of all seniority (and therefore his committee chair). In July, 1969, the Supreme Court ruled that the House had violated the Constitution in its 1967 vote to bar him from his Congressional seat. His health failing, Powell retired to Bimini in 1971, after losing the Democratic primary for his Congressional seat.

R

RAYBURN, Samuel Taliaferro (1882–1961). Aptly known as Mr. Speaker, Rayburn fulfilled a boyhood ambition to be Speaker of the House of Representatives, serving in that post for over 17 years, longer than any other Congressman. Rayburn was born in Tennessee and grew up in northeast Texas, where he helped on his father's 40-acre cotton farm. By working at odd jobs and as a teacher, he earned a degree at East Texas Normal School (now East Texas State University) in 1904. Rayburn was elected to the Texas legislature in 1906, the first of 28 consecutive election campaigns he waged without defeat. While studying law at the University of Texas, he served three terms in the legislature (1907–1912), the last term as the Speaker of the Texas House of Representatives. At 30, Rayburn was elected to the first of his 25 terms (1913–1961) in the U.S. House of Representatives and soon earned the respect of President Woodrow Wilson (1856–1924). Later, as chairman of the Interstate and Foreign Commerce Committee from 1931 to 1937, he sponsored many of the New Deal measures of President Franklin D. Roosevelt (1882–1945). He became Speaker on September 16, 1940. Except for four years when the Republicans controlled Congress (1947–1949 and 1953–1955), Rayburn held the post until his death, doubling the

Samuel T. Rayburn

previous record held by Henry Clay (1777–1852), who was Speaker for over eight years. During the administration of **Harry S. Truman** (*see*), Rayburn opposed Truman's efforts to regulate natural-gas and oil producers. However, he backed Truman's foreign-aid and trade policies, including the Marshall Plan (*see* **Truman Doctrine**). In 1957, together with his protégé, Senate majority leader Lyndon B. Johnson (1908–1973) of Texas, Rayburn effectively worked with President **Dwight D. Eisenhower** (*see*) in enacting the first major civil-rights act since the Reconstruction era. Rayburn's control in the House was based on his ability to conciliate and compromise. "Persuasion and reason are the only way to lead them. In that way the Speaker has influence and power in the House," he said. Chairman at the Democratic National Conventions in 1948, 1952, and 1956, Rayburn declined that role in 1960 to back Johnson for the Presidency. However, when **John F. Kennedy** (*see*) won the nomination and then the election, Rayburn

fought to overcome conservative opposition to the new President's legislative program. "I always say without prefix, without suffix, and without apology," he declared, "that I am a Democrat." Although he failed to rally support for a broad federal aid-to-education bill, Rayburn was successful in winning early support for Kennedy's liberal housing, minimum-wage, and urban-renewal programs.

REUTHER, Walter Philip (1907–1970). One of the founders of the Congress of Industrial Organizations (C.I.O.) in the 1930s, Reuther successfully opposed Communist infiltration in the 1940s and helped organize the merger of the C.I.O. with the American Federation of Labor (A.F.L.) in 1955. Articulate and scrupulously honest, Reuther, the son of a German-born labor organizer, was born in Wheeling, West Virginia. Although he went to work at the age of 15, he later completed high school and attended Wayne State University in Detroit in his spare time. At 16, he led his first protest, against the Wheeling Steel Corporation, whose seven-day work week prevented him from taking part in his family's Sunday-afternoon discussions of current issues. The protest cost him his 40-cents-an-hour job. Two years later, Reuther became a shop foreman in a Ford Motor Company plant in Detroit. Discharged by Ford in 1932 for his union activities, Reuther worked briefly in mines and factories in England and spent more than a year in a Ford-built automotive plant in the Soviet Union, where working conditions and the Communist system appalled him. Reuther returned to Detroit and became active in the early organizing of the United Automobile Workers of America (U.A.W.). He led one of the first U.A.W. sit-down strikes in 1936. After he became vice-president of the U.A.W. in 1942, Reuther devised the plan that converted automobile factories to the

Walter R. Reuther (second from right) at the Ford Motor Company plant in Dearborn, Michigan where, in 1932, violence flared between striking plant workers and Dearborn police.

manufacture of airplanes in World War II. After the war, as president of the U.A.W. and a vice-president of the C.I.O., he led successful strikes to gain cost-of-living increases, pension plans, and other benefits for workers. He denounced Communists within the C.I.O., declaring that they had no right "to peddle the Communist Party line with a C.I.O. label on the wrapper." In April, 1948, a shotgun blast from an unidentified assailant severely wounded Reuther, and an unsuccessful attempt to dynamite the U.A.W. offices was made in December, 1949. In November, 1952, on the deaths of presidents Philip Murray (1886–1952) of the C.I.O. and William Green (1873–1952) of the A.F.L., an opportunity arose to draw the two federations closer together. Their new presidents, Reuther of the C.I.O. and **George Meany** (*see*) of the A.F.L., began in April, 1953, to work out a series of agreements that resulted in a formal merger in December, 1955. Meany was elected president of the com-

bined A.F.L.-C.I.O., while Reuther became vice-president in charge of the industrial division. In December, 1966, Reuther's U.A.W. accused the A.F.L.-C.I.O. of failing to fulfill the merger aims. Three months later he resigned from the executive council of the A.F.L.-C.I.O. because he disagreed with the council's support of the Vietnam War. The recipient of numerous awards and honorary degrees, Reuther was named in 1968 the "greatest living U.S. labor leader" by 48 newspaper editors.

RICKOVER, Hyman George (1900–1986). A pioneer in the development of atomic sea power, Rickover is known as the father of the nuclear submarine. As a child, he came to America from Russia with his family in 1905. After graduating from Annapolis in 1922, he served five years' duty at sea before returning there to study electrical engineering. In 1929, he earned a master's degree from Columbia University. The following year, Rickover received submarine training at

New London, Connecticut. In 1939, he was assigned to the Bureau of Ships in Washington, D.C., and during World War II served as head of its electrical section. At the end of the war, Rickover joined the Atomic Energy Commission's Manhattan Project at Oak Ridge, Tennessee, which took part in developing the atomic bomb. He planned the construction of the first nuclear-powered submarine, the *Nautilus*, which was launched in 1954. To facilitate cooperation between the A.E.C. and the Navy, Rickover was made chief of the Naval Reactors Branch of the A.E.C. and head of the Nuclear Propulsion Division of the Navy's Bureau of Ships. His civilian post, however, brought the outspoken naval officer into conflict with his superiors. When the Navy did not promote Captain Rickover to an admiral's rank in 1951 and 1952, he faced compulsory retirement, until Congress pressured the Navy into making him a rear admiral in 1953. In 1961, President **John F. Kennedy** (*see*) ordered the Navy to keep

Rickover beyond the official retirement age. That same year he received the Distinguished Service Medal for his "skillful technical direction, unusual foresight, and unswerving perseverance" in the field of naval nuclear propulsion. Rickover published two books on education, *Education and Freedom* (1959) and *Swiss Schools and Ours: Why Theirs Are Better* (1962). Although officially retired in 1964, Rickover remained active in the Navy until 1982, when he called for an end to nuclear weapons and nuclear power and truly retired.

ROBINSON, Jack Roosevelt ("Jackie") (1910–1972).

The first black major-league baseball player, Robinson became a symbol of achievement for the civil-rights movement. The Georgia-born athlete was raised in Pasadena, California, and starred in basketball, football, baseball, and track at the University of California from 1939 to 1941. During World War II, Robinson served as a second lieutenant in the 27th Cavalry. After the war, playing shortstop for the Kansas City Monarchs in the Negro American Baseball League, he attracted the attention of Branch Rickey (1881–1965), president of the Brooklyn Dodgers. In 1945, Rickey signed him to play with the Montreal Royals, a Dodger farm club. During his first season, Robinson faced discrimination and hostility, but stole 40 bases, and led the league with a .349 batting average. In 1947, he moved up to the Brooklyn Dodgers. As the first black player, Robinson endured verbal and physical attacks by players and fans alike, but the versatile second baseman won grudging respect and the Major League's Rookie of the Year Award that season. In 1949, he was named the National League's Most Valuable Player, and his .342 average led the league. When he retired in 1956 after ten seasons with the Dodgers, Robinson had compiled an overall batting average of .311. Six years

Jackie Robinson

later, he was elected to the National Baseball Hall of Fame, the first black so honored. Robinson became a vice-president of a chain of coffee shops. He also contributed a sports column to *The New York Post* in 1959. In 1964, he served as deputy director of the unsuccessful campaign of New York Governor Nelson Rockefeller (1908–1979) for the Republican Presidential nomination. Robinson, who remained a civil-

rights activist throughout his life, later served as Rockefeller's special assistant for community affairs and became chairman of the board of the National Freedom Bank in New York City.

ROSENBERG SPY CASE.

On June 19, 1953, in New York's Sing Sing Prison, Julius Rosenberg (1918–1953) and his wife, Ethel (1921–1953), became the first American civilians executed for treason, the result of one of the most spectacular spy cases in American history. Beginning in 1940, Rosenberg, then an engineer with the U.S. Army Signal Corps, and his wife started selling American military information to Soviet agents. In 1944–45, they turned over vital information—obtained from Mrs. Rosenberg's brother, David Greenglass (born 1922), an army sergeant and foreman of an atomic assembly plant at Los Alamos, New Mexico—concerning the atomic bomb. Greenglass stole sketches of the detonating device and other parts of the atom bomb that was dropped on Naga-

Spies Julius and Ethel Rosenberg posed a few days before their execution.

saki, Japan, in August, 1945. Earlier, in February of that year, Rosenberg was suspended from the army for belonging to the Communist Party. In 1950, the FBI (*see* **Hoover, J. Edgar**) charged both Rosenbergs with conspiracy to disclose secrets to the Soviet Union. Their widely publicized trial opened on March 6, 1951. On April 5, they were found guilty of treason under the Espionage Act of 1917, which made the death sentence mandatory. Greenglass, who was the government's chief witness, testified that the Rosenbergs had turned over nuclear plans to Harry Gold (born 1910), a Philadelphia chemist, who was the contact man and courier between the couple and Soviet agents. Anatoli Yakovlev, a Soviet agent and former vice-consul in New York City, who had fled to the U.S.S.R. in December, 1946, was indicted in absentia at the same time as the Rosenbergs. Gold received a 30-year prison sentence in December, 1950, for his part in the conspiracy. Gold was also associated with two Soviet agents in Britain, Alan Nunn May (born 1911), a scientist, and Dr. Klaus Fuchs (born 1911), a German-born atomic physicist who had worked at Los Alamos in 1945. Both May and Fuchs received prison sentences in Great Britain. Another member of the spy ring, Morton Sobell (born 1917), an electronic engineer, was sentenced to 30 years in prison. The trial provoked worldwide interest, and many non-Communists, including various religious leaders, believed the Rosenbergs' sentence of death too severe and urged clemency. Despite numerous motions for a retrial, several stays of execution, and two appeals to President **Dwight D. Eisenhower** (*see*), the last one on the day before their execution, all attempts to save them failed. After his release by the British in 1953, May went to Ghana to teach, while Fuchs, freed in 1959, settled in East Germany. Gold was paroled in 1965, four years before Sobell.

Greenglass, rewarded for his cooperation with only a 15-year sentence, was released in 1960.

RUSK, (David) Dean (born 1909). As Secretary of State under Presidents **John F. Kennedy** (*see*) and Lyndon B. Johnson (1908–1973), Rusk was one of the leading proponents of American policy in Vietnam. Born in Georgia, Rusk graduated from North Carolina's Davidson College in 1933, won a Rhodes Scholarship, and earned a master's degree from Oxford University in Great Britain in 1934. He then taught at Mills College in California and became dean of the faculty in 1938. After completing his legal training at the University of California, Rusk was assigned to army intelligence early in World War II, and later became deputy chief of staff to General Joseph Stilwell (1883–1946). After the war, Rusk joined the State Department, serving briefly as a delegate to the United Nations before being named Assistant Secretary of State for United Nations affairs in 1949. As Assistant Secretary of State for Far Eastern affairs in 1950, Rusk played a major role in deliberations leading to U.S. involvement in the Korean War. He believed that intervention would prevent further Communist aggression in the Far East, but he later supported President **Harry S.**

Dean Rusk

Truman (*see*) in recalling General Douglas MacArthur (1880–1964). In 1951, Rusk assisted Secretary of State **John Foster Dulles** (*see*) in negotiating a peace treaty with Japan. In 1952, he became president of the Rockefeller Foundation, directing the distribution of funds— about $250,000,000 in all—for various projects, including aid to other nations. He resigned in 1960, when President-elect Kennedy named him Secretary of State. Under Kennedy, Rusk stressed a need for the "quiet diplomacy" of trained specialists, rather than well-publicized summit meetings between heads of state. He emphasized the importance of aiding underdeveloped nations and backed Kennedy's aim to negotiate with the Communists from a position of strength. He advised Kennedy during the ill-fated **Bay of Pigs Invasion** (*see*) in Cuba, and in May, 1961, Rusk helped negotiate a cease-fire after a threatened Communist take-over in Laos. After Kennedy's assassination in 1963, President Johnson asked Rusk to stay in his post. In 1964, he promoted a massive buildup of American military forces in Vietnam, "to see to it that North Vietnam does not seize South Vietnam by force." He denied the existence of much ground fighting, although more than 350,000 American soldiers were stationed there. In 1967, Senator Strom Thurmond (born 1902) of South Carolina accused Rusk of inadequate efforts to win the war. The Secretary responded that the use of nuclear weapons was unjustifiable. "We have to try to find a reasonable and rational way to do what is required to stop aggression," he declared. Rusk left office in January, 1969, and a year later accepted a teaching position at the University of Georgia.

S

SABIN, Albert. *See* **Salk, Jonas** and **Sabin, Albert.**

Jonas Salk

SALK, Jonas Edward (born 1914) and **SABIN, Albert Bruce** (born 1906). Working independently, Jonas Salk and Albert Sabin developed the vaccines now used to prevent the once-dreaded disease of poliomyelitis, commonly known as polio. Polio, a virus that primarily attacks children fifteen years old or younger, causes inflammation in the spinal cord, often resulting in paralysis and weakening of the limbs and lungs, with death a frequent result. During a 1952 epidemic, it attacked more than 20,000 people, frightening the entire United States. Dr. Jonas Salk, born and educated in New York City, joined in the search for a vaccine against polio in the late 1940s. Working at the University of Pittsburgh, he grew the virus in a laboratory culture, killed it with a chemical, and derived a vaccine from the killed virus. In 1953, Salk reported early successful tests of his vaccine. By 1955, extensive government testing had established it as a safe and effective agent against the disease. When injected into the bloodstream, the vaccine stimulates a person's body to produce enough antibodies against polio to render him or her immune to the disease for life. Several years later, Dr. Albert Sabin, a researcher at the University of Cincinnati, achieved another significant breakthrough in the battle against polio. Born in Poland, Sabin had immigrated with his family to New Jersey, and had been educated in New York City. In the mid-1950s, he developed a vaccine that could be taken orally instead of by injection. Sabin's vaccine—cultivated from living polio virus that had been attenuated, or weakened—was much cheaper and easier to distribute than Salk's had been. Like Salk's vaccine, Sabin's oral vaccine makes people immune to polio by stimulating the body's production of antibodies. After beginning extensive testing in 1957, the United States government declared Sabin's vaccine safe and effective in 1961. The Salk and Sabin vaccines allayed the fear of polio that had plagued most Americans. Although the disease continues to afflict many people in the world's developing countries—where such medicines are still not readily available—the vaccines virtually eliminated polio in the United States. After their success against the polio virus, both Salk and Sabin continued to work on infectious diseases: Salk became a founding director of the Salk Institute for Biological Studies in California; Sabin has conducted research at the University of Cincinnati and South Carolina, and has served as a consultant to international health organizations.

SANDBURG, Carl (1878–1967). One of America's most famous and best-loved poets, Sandburg was also a folk singer and the author of a definitive six-volume biography of Abraham Lincoln (1809–1865). This masterpiece—*Abraham Lincoln: The Prairie Years* (1926, two volumes) and *Abraham Lincoln: The War Years* (1939, four volumes)—which required years of research, depicts Lincoln as the embodiment of the American democratic spirit. It won Sandburg the Pulitzer Prize for History in 1940. Born in Galesburg, Illinois, Sandburg attended public school until he was 13. After serving in Puerto Rico during the Spanish-American War, he attended Lombard College (now Knox College) in Galesburg from 1898–1902, but never graduated. He later worked as a newspaperman in Milwaukee, Wisconsin, and as secretary from 1910 to 1912 to that city's Socialist mayor, Emil Seidel (1864–1947). Sandburg continued his journalistic career in Chicago, where he enjoyed his first poetic success in 1914, when several of his poems appeared in *Poetry* magazine. In "Chicago," he caught the throbbing energy of that metropolis, describing it as

> Hog Butcher for the World,
> Tool Maker, Stacker of Wheat,
> Player with Railroads and the
>   Nation's Freight Handler;
> Stormy, husky, brawling,
> City of the Big Shoulders.

"Chicago" was also the title piece of his volume, *Chicago Poems* (1916), which with *Cornhuskers* (1918, winner of a special Pulitzer award in 1919), and *Smoke and Steel* (1920), established Sandburg's reputation as one of the nation's most original and vital poets. His

Carl Sandburg

free-form verses captured the American idiom—especially the rugged Middle Western speech—and contained many lyrical passages. During the 1920s and 1930s, Sandburg traveled all over the country, reading his poetry and singing folk songs, accompanying himself on the guitar. He published two collections of local ballads, *The American Songbag* (1927) and *The New American Songbag* (1950). Sandburg's later volumes of poetry included *Complete Poems* (1950, winner of the Pulitzer Prize for Poetry in 1951) and *Harvest Poems, 1910–1960* (1960). He also wrote several children's books, such as *Rootabaga Stories* (1922); some prose works, including *Steichen the Photographer* (1929), a biography of his brother-in-law Edward Steichen (1879–1973); and *Remembrance Rock* (1948), a novel.

SOUND BARRIER. In 1947, Chuck Yeager became the first man to fly faster than the speed of sound. Six years later, Jacqueline Cochran (1910–1980) became the first woman to match that feat. After the development of the jet engine in the 1940s, test pilots in the United States and abroad began attempting to exceed the speed of sound, or Mach I as this speed is technically called. However, the resistance of the air, which increases dramatically as the speed of sound is approached, often caused planes to vibrate uncontrollably and crash. This recurring phenomenon led some to refer to Mach I as the "sound barrier." In 1947, the Air Force chose Chuck Yeager, who had flown numerous combat missions as a World War II pilot, to test its new rocket jet airplane, the *Bell X–1*, which was specifically designed for supersonic flight. The test, performed at Muroc Air Field in California, took place on October 14, 1947, with Yeager concealing the fact that he had broken two ribs in a recent fall from a horse. Switching to the plane's rocket engines one by one, he accelerated the craft and

broke Mach I at 42,000 feet, creating a sonic boom heard by Air Force observers on the field below. Six years after Yeager first broke the sound barrier, Jacqueline Cochran became the first woman to fly at supersonic speed. An orphan who had been raised by a poor foster family, Cochran had earned money by selling cosmetics before she became a pilot in 1932. After heading a U.S. military pilot-training program for women in World War II, she founded and managed her own cosmetics firm. In 1953, piloting a F-86 Sabre jet fighter plane over Edwards Air Force Base in California, Cochran became the first woman to break the sound barrier, pulling out of a number of steep dives at supersonic speed. Yeager and Cochran continued flying and setting records throughout the 1950s and 1960s. In 1953, Yeager flew another experimental plane at the speed of 1,650 mph—a record at that time. Cochran went on to set more than 200 flying records.

SOUTHEAST ASIA TREATY ORGANIZATION. Primarily designed to block Communist expansion in Asia after the **Korean War** (*see*), SEATO was created in 1954 by the United States, Great Britain, France, Australia, New Zealand, Pakistan, Thailand, and the Philippines. President **Dwight D. Eisenhower**, his Secretary of State, **John Foster Dulles** (*see both*), British Prime Minster Winston Churchill (1874–1965), and Churchill's foreign secretary, Anthony Eden (1897–1973), drew up the SEATO provisions and, on September 8, 1954, at Manila, the eight-member nations signed the Southeast Asia Collective Defense Treaty, which became effective on February 19, 1955. The treaty area covered Southeast Asia, including the territories of its members, and the southwest Pacific. It specifically excluded, however, both Formosa (Taiwan) and the British colony of Hong Kong. Vietnam, Cambodia, and Laos—all

part of French Indochina before 1954—were accorded military protection under the treaty, although they were not members. A defensive alignment, SEATO, unlike the **North Atlantic Treaty Organization** (*see*), had no military units directly attached to it. Collective security was guaranteed under the treaty in the case of an attack on any of the member nations. Disagreements with the United States over the Vietnam War by Britain, France, and other nations weakened the organization, and on June 30, 1977, SEATO was officially disbanded.

SPACE FLIGHT. The selection of seven men to become the country's first astronauts in 1959 officially inaugurated the U.S. manned space program that would capture the imagination of the world and culminate in the landing of a man on the moon ten years later. The U.S. commitment to space exploration had accelerated with the launching of *Sputnik 1*—the first satellite artificially placed into orbit around the earth—by the Soviet Union on October 4, 1957. Less than a month later, on November 3, the Soviets launched a second satellite, *Sputnik 2*, which carried a dog named Laika into orbit. The United States, facing this sudden challenge to its long-held assumption of scientific and technological superiority, responded quickly with the launching of *Explorer 1*, the first U.S. satellite, on February 1, 1958. Instruments abroad *Explorer 1* transmitted data to earth that led to an important scientific discovery: a belt of electrically charged particles that surround the earth, now known as the Van Allen radiation belt. On July 29, 1958, President **Dwight D. Eisenhower** (*see*) approved the National Aeronautics and Space Act, which created the National Aeronautics and Space Administration (NASA), a civilian agency intended to match and surpass Soviet achievements in space. NASA, in charge of planning and overseeing the United States's space program, immediately initiated Project Mercury, the nation's first manned space flight venture. Further accomplishments by the Soviet Union in 1959, including a satellite that passed the moon, another that struck the moon, and a third that transmitted photographs of the far side of the moon back to earth, added greater urgency to NASA's work as it tested the Saturn rocket engines that would eventually power the Mercury spacecraft. Later that year, NASA announced the names of the first seven astronauts, all former officers in the U.S. Air Force or Navy: Alan B. Shepard, Jr. (born 1923), Virgil I. Grissom (1926–1967), John H. Glenn, Jr. (born 1921), M. Scott Carpenter (born 1925), Walter M. Schirra, Jr. (born 1923), L. Gordon Cooper, Jr. (born 1927), and Donald K. Slayton (born 1924). On June 3, 1959, NASA began construction of Saturn launch facilities at Cape Canaveral, Florida (known as Cape Kennedy from 1963, when President **John F. Kennedy** (*see*) was assassinated, until 1973). NASA had laid the groundwork and turned to President Eisenhower for final approval of the Apollo Project, dedicated to achieving lunar orbit by a peopled spacecraft by 1969. Eisenhower—after consulting with his Science Advisory Committee, which viewed the proposal as cost-prohibitive and advised that space flight could not be "justified on purely scientific grounds"—stunned NASA by refusing the request. Upon taking office in 1961, President Kennedy quickly reversed his predecessor's decision, a decision that was made even more urgent when Soviet cosmonaut Yuri A. Gagarin (1934–1968), aboard *Vostok 1* on April 12, became the first person to orbit the earth. Less than a month later, on May 5, Alan Shepard was launched on a successful suborbital flight aboard the *Freedom 7*, one of the Project Mercury spacecraft. With the President's approval, NASA accelerated Project Mercury: On Feb-

ruary 20, 1962, John Glenn became the first American to orbit the earth, and by 1963, when the last Project Mercury spacecraft was launched (achieving a U.S. record at that time of over 34 hours in space), six of the seven original astronauts had successfully piloted solo missions in space. (Discovery of a heart ailment prevented the seventh, Donald Slayton, from flying in space until the monumental Soviet-American linkup of *Apollo* and *Soyuz* spacecraft in 1975.) In endorsing Project Mercury, President Kennedy made it clear that he saw it as an essential first step toward a manned landing on the moon, which would not only increase the nation's prestige, but also lead to great advances in scientific knowledge about the earth's nearest neighbor. On May 25, 1961, shortly after Shepard's safe return to earth, Kennedy had proclaimed that "Now it is time . . . for this nation to take a clearly leading role in space achievement, which in many ways may hold the key to our future on earth." He urged the nation to "commit itself to achieving the goal, before this decade is out, of landing a man on the moon and returning him safely to earth."

STEVENSON, Adlai Ewing (1900–1965). Twice the unsuccessful Democratic Presidential candidate in the 1950s, Stevenson became a leading world statesman and the chief spokesman for the United States in the United Nations. The grandson of Vice-President Adlai E. Stevenson (1835–1914), Stevenson was born in California, the son of a newspaper and mining executive, and raised in his parents' hometown of Bloomington, Illinois. After graduating from Princeton in 1922 and from Northwestern University Law School, he joined a Chicago law firm in 1927. In 1931, he served as special counsel for the Agricultural Adjustment Administration and later the Federal Alcohol Control Administration. In the late 1930s, as war

broke out in Europe, Stevenson spoke out against isolationism. From July, 1941, to April, 1944, he served in Europe as a special assistant to the Secretary of the Navy. In February, 1945, Stevenson returned to Washington as an assistant to the Secretary of State, Edward R. Stettinius, Jr. (1900–1949), and helped plan the charter meeting of the United Nations in San Francisco. He was a delegate at the second and third General Assembly sessions in New York in 1946 and 1947. Stevenson decided to seek the governorship of Illinois in 1948 and won with a plurality of 572,067 votes. As governor, he instituted major reforms, including cleaning up the corrupt state-police force, smashing gambling interests, reorganizing mental hospitals, doubling aid to schools, modernizing the highway system, and abolishing nearly 1,300 unnecessary state jobs. By 1952, Stevenson had become a prominent figure in Democratic circles. In July, at the Democratic National Convention, Stevenson was drafted as the party's Presidential candidate on the third ballot. Stevenson, an articulate and urbane intellectual who lost large blocks of votes because of his uncompromising candor, was pitted against **Dwight D. Eisenhower** (*see*), whose great national popularity had prompted both the Democratic and Republican parties to seek him as a candidate. Stevenson polled about 27,000,000 popular votes against Eisenhower's almost 34,000,000 and won only 89 electoral votes to Eisenhower's 442. Stevenson campaigned actively for the Democratic party in the Congressional elections of 1954. Charging that the Republican Party was "half McCarthy and half Eisenhower," (*see* **Joseph R. McCarthy**), Stevenson was accused by Eisenhower's Vice-President, Richard M. Nixon (born 1913), of unconsciously spreading Communist propaganda. In 1956, Stevenson was renominated by the Democrats for President, beating out **Estes Kefauver** (*see*) of

Tennessee and New York Governor Averell Harriman (born 1891). Eisenhower ridiculed Stevenson's request for an end to above-ground nuclear testing as a "moratorium on common sense," although in 1958, the former general would echo the request. Stevenson was again defeated—this time polling only 73 electoral votes to Eisenhower's 457. Stevenson became a belated candidate in the 1960 Democratic convention but lost to **John F. Kennedy** (*see*). As Kennedy's ambassador to the United Nations, Stevenson, once an advocate of admitting Communist China to the United Nations, reversed his stand to conform with Kennedy's foreign policy. His logic and language proved valuable in the U.N. debates. The **Bay of Pigs Invasion** (*see*) in 1961 embarrassed Stevenson, who had not been adequately briefed by the President about the United States's involvement. He later defended the American position in the Cuban missile crisis in October, 1962. After Kennedy's assassination, President Lyndon B. Johnson (1908–1973) reconfirmed Stevenson's appointment. In July, 1965, he confided to friends his intention to resign soon. A few days later, he suffered a heart attack on a London street and died.

T

TAFT, Robert Alphonso (1889–1953). "Mr. Republican"—as this Ohio Senator was called—was known for his conservatism, isolationist principles, and personal integrity. The eldest son of William Howard Taft (1857–1930), the 27th President of the United States, Taft was born in Cincinnati and graduated from Yale in 1910. After earning his law degree at Harvard, he practiced in Cincinnati and, during World War I, served as counsel for the U.S. Food Administration and the American Relief Administration in Europe. In 1921, Taft was elected

Robert A. Taft

to the Ohio legislature (1921–1926 and 1931–1932). He was elected to the first of three terms (1939–1953) in the U.S. Senate in 1938. In Congress, Taft opposed the New Deal programs of President Franklin D. Roosevelt (1882–1945) and led the isolationists, believing that a negotiated peace with Nazi government was still possible after Germany began World War II in Europe. However, when the Japanese attacked Pearl Harbor on December 7, 1941, he backed America's war effort. Taft reverted to his isolationist stance in his campaign for the 1948 Republican Presidential nomination, opposing both the Marshall Plan (*see* **Truman Doctrine**) and the **North Atlantic Treaty Organization** (*see*). At the same time, he advocated strengthening the authority of the United Nations. Taft became best known for drafting and cosponsoring the controversial Labor-Management Relations Act, which became known as the **Taft-Hartley Act** (*see*). Passed by Congress in June, 1947, over the veto of President **Harry S. Truman** (*see*), the act was designed to curtail the power of labor unions and make them subject to government control. After failing in his bids for Republican Presidential nomination in both 1940 and 1948, Taft made a final attempt in 1952. Although he was initially backed by party professionals, the

drive to nominate General **Dwight D. Eisenhower** (*see*), a national hero, gained momentum and delegate strength. In Chicago that summer, a change in convention rules on the seating of contested delegates worked to Eisenhower's benefit. As a result, Eisenhower won 595 votes to Taft's 500 on the first ballot and, when Minnesota switched its votes, Eisenhower won the nomination. After a reconciliation, Taft became a trusted adviser to Eisenhower, who was elected President over Democrat **Adlai E. Stevenson** (*see*). Taft also exerted a wide influence as Senate majority leader. However, in June, 1953, he disclosed that he had a serious illness and resigned from the Senate leadership. He died soon afterward of cancer. A 100-foot-tall Taft Memorial Bell Tower, situated near the Capitol, was dedicated in his honor in 1959.

TAFT-HARTLEY ACT. Enacted on June 23, 1947, over the veto of President **Harry S Truman** (*see*) and despite the opposition of organized labor, the Taft-Hartley Act limited the conduct of unions in labor-management disputes. The provisions of the bill, officially known as the Labor-Management Relations Act, amended the National Labor Relations Act (Wagner Act) of 1935 that had placed restrictions on management. The Taft-Hartley Act authorized the federal government to issue an 80-day injunction against any strike that would endanger the "national health or safety." It prohibited direct union contributions to political campaigns, and required public disclosure of a union's financial records. In addition, the act banned the closed shop, permitted employers to sue unions for broken contracts and unfair labor practices, required unions to give 60 days' notice of their intent to strike, and required union leaders to file loyalty oaths—affidavits that they were not Communists. An especially controversial provision permitted states to enact right-to-work laws, allowing workers to hold a job without being required to join a union. Two Republicans sponsored the measure: Senator **Robert A. Taft** (*see*) of Ohio and Representative Fred A. Hartley, Jr. (1902–1969) of New Jersey. Republican victories in the Congressional elections of 1946 enabled the House to override Truman's veto by a vote of 331 to 83, and by a Senate vote of 68 to 25. Union leaders, condemning the act as a "slave bill," campaigned for its repeal and backed Truman in 1948, despite his inability to win Congressional approval of repeal. The Landrum-Griffin Bill of 1959 repealed the section of the Taft-Hartley Act requiring loyalty oaths from union leaders. In 1965, President Lyndon B. Johnson urged repeal of Section 14-b. A bill, passed in the House of Representatives, was blocked by a filibuster in the Senate, led by Republican Senator **Everett M. Dirksen** (*see*) of Illinois. Right-to-work laws are still in effect in many states.

TRUMAN, Harry S. (*Continued from Volume 15*). With the end of World War II, the man thrust into the Presidency by the death of Franklin D. Roosevelt (1882–1945) faced complex domestic problems and steadily increasing tensions between the United States and the Soviet Union. On August 18, 1945—four days after Japan's surrender—Truman extended wartime controls on production, wages, and prices. In September, before an unreceptive Congress, Truman outlined his domestic program, later termed the Fair Deal: federal aid to education, an increased minimum wage, a medical-insurance plan, and civil-rights legislation. By 1946, nearly 2,000,000 people were unemployed, and labor unions were striking for higher wages. Truman's determination to prevent strikes led to frequent confrontations with **John L. Lewis** (*see*), head of the United Mine Workers, and other labor leaders. In May, 1946, Truman revealed

Truman played the piano for the Kennedys at 1961 White House dinner.

plans to draft striking railroad workers into the Army and force them to run the trains. The railroad union called off its planned strike. Truman, however, vetoed the antilabor Case Bill in 1946 and the **Taft-Hartley Act** (*see*) in 1947. Truman's position on price controls alienated business leaders and his civil-rights proposals antagonized the South. The Congressional elections of 1946 produced the first Republican-controlled Congress since 1930. Meanwhile, Truman's attention became increasingly occupied with foreign affairs. The basic idea behind his foreign policy—the so-called **Truman Doctrine** (*see*)—was the containment of Communism, and he requested billions of dollars in Congressional appropriations toward that end. The Soviet Union challenged Truman by blocking Allied access to Berlin in June, 1948, but the **Berlin Airlift** (*see*) forced the U.S.S.R. to back down. Truman's decision, in 1948, to seek his own four-year term was not a popular one, even within his own party. Left-wing Democrats organized a third party and nominated Henry A. Wallace (1888–1965) for President. The South, opposing Truman's insistence on a civil-rights plank in the Democratic platform, nominated Strom Thurmond (born 1902) on the States' Rights ticket. The remaining Democrats nominated Truman and chose Senator

Alben W. Barkley (1877–1956) of Kentucky as his running mate. During his whistle-stop campaign, the crowds frequently shouted, "Give 'em hell, Harry!" The polls, however, forecast a landslide victory for Republican **Thomas E. Dewey** (*see*). In his upset victory, Truman won the labor and farm vote and polled 303 electoral votes to Dewey's 189 and Thurmond's 39. Truman won 24,000,000 popular votes, 2,000,000 more than Dewey. The Democrats also gained control of Congress, allowing Truman to see many of his Fair Deal proposals become law. He also desegregated the armed forces by executive order. As in his first term, Truman concentrated on foreign affairs. The **North Atlantic Treaty Organization** (*see*) was established in 1949 to resist Communist aggression in Europe, a menace that loomed large after the Soviet Union exploded an atomic bomb that year and China fell to Communists led by Mao Tse-tung (1893–1976). Meanwhile, the House Un-American Activities Committee, which Truman called "the most un-American activity in the whole government," had started a search for Communists in America. The case of **Alger Hiss** (*see*) and the **Rosenberg spy case** (*see*) heightened the hysteria. The McCarran Internal Security Act, passed over Truman's veto in September, 1950, required all members of the Communist Party and of Communist-front organizations to register with the Attorney General. It also prohibited aliens who had been Communists from working in defense plants, and authorized the President to hold them in detention camps in the event of war. Truman believed the act was unconstitutional. During the **Korean War** (*see*), Truman made one of his most difficult and controversial decisions: relieving General Douglas MacArthur (1880–1964) of command. Later, Truman explained, "General MacArthur was insubordinate and I fired him. That's all there was to it.'' On November 1, 1950, two Puerto Rican nationalists tried to assassinate Truman at Blair House, where he was living while the White House, across the street, was being renovated. Although Truman was not injured, a Secret Serviceman and one of the assailants were killed. The surviving attacker was sentenced to death, but Truman commuted the sentence to life imprisonment. In March, 1952, Truman announced that he would not be a candidate for reelection. In January, 1953, Truman returned to his home in Independence, Missouri, where he founded the Truman Library (1957). He published three volumes of memoirs, *Years of Decision* (1955), *Years of Trial and Hope* (1956), and *Mr. Citizen* (1960). Truman died in 1972.

TRUMAN DOCTRINE. As the first step in his program to contain the influence of Communism, President **Harry S. Truman** (*see*) told a joint session of Congress on March 12, 1947: ''I believe that it must be the policy of the United States to support free peoples who are resisting attempted subjugation by armed minorities or by outside pressures. I believe that we must assist free peoples to work out their own destinies in their own way.'' This bold foreign policy statement has since been called the Truman Doctrine. The President's request for $400,000,000 to assist Greece and Turkey in resisting Communism was passed by Congress on May 22 after considerable debate. Initially, the Truman Doctrine was restricted to nations where there was danger of a Communist take-over. However, on June 5, 1947, in a commencement address at Harvard, Secretary of State George C. Marshall (188–1959) warned that a stable European economy was essential to America's security. He suggested that U.S. policy should be directed against ''hunger, poverty, desperation, and chaos. Its purpose should be the revival of a working economy in the

world.'' Thus, the European Recovery Program, or Marshall Plan, became an extension of the Truman Doctrine, offering economic aid to all nations. The Soviet Union immediately denounced the Marshall Plan as meddling in the internal affairs of other nations. But France and Great Britain organized a conference of sixteen nations—Britain, France, Austria, Belgium, Denmark, Greece, Iceland, Ireland, Italy, Luxembourg, the Netherlands, Norway, Portugal, Sweden, Switzerland, and Turkey—to formulate a program. They estimated that with $19.3 billion from America and an additional $3.1 billion from the International Bank, they could achieve stability and self-sufficiency by 1951. In December, 1947, Truman recommended that Congress appropriate $17 billion over a five-year period to ensure the permanent recovery of Europe's economy. A Communist coup in Czechoslovakia in February, 1948, sped the passage of the bill. Within three years, America spent more than $12 billion in foreign aid, and a thriving Western Europe proved a formidable barrier against further Communist gains. The Four Point Program, outlined in Truman's inaugural address on January 20, 1949, aimed at lending technical assistance to underdeveloped countries. The initial appropriation was passed by Congress in September, 1950, after the outbreak of the **Korean War** (*see*). Eventually, 54 nations took advantage of the program, which was administered by the Technical Cooperation Administration. Under President **Dwight D. Eisenhower** (*see*) the program was integrated into the overall foreign-aid program.

TWENTY-SECOND AMENDMENT. Proposed in March, 1947, less than three years after Franklin D. Roosevelt (1882–1945) had won his fourth election to the Presidency, the 22nd Amendment to the United States Constitution has limited all Presidents since **Harry S. Truman**

(*see*) to a maximum of two terms or ten years in office. The Amendment aroused considerable Congressional debate before its approval by both the Senate amd the House of Representatives. Republicans, distressed by the four-time election of Roosevelt, a Democrat, strongly supported the limitation. The Amendment's opponents claimed that barring re-elected Presidents from seeking a third term would result in ''lame duck'' Presidencies. The Amendment, they argued, would not only diminish second-term Presidents' accountability for their actions, but also reduce their power to accomplish desired programs during the second term. However, still others argued that the Amendment would provide a needed additional check on the power of the President. With the approval of the 36th state in 1951, the Amendment met the requirement of ratification by three quarters of the 48 states (Alaska and Hawaii had not yet become states) and became law on March 1, 1951.

U

THE U-2 INCIDENT. On May 1, 1960, the already strained relations between the United States and the Soviet Union worsened with the capture of American pilot Francis Gary Powers (1929–1977), whose high-altitude U-2 plane was shot down by the Russians 1,200 miles within their borders. At his trial for espionage in Moscow, Powers confessed that he had been flying a reconnaisance mission to map Soviet military targets for the Central Intelligence Agency. At first, U.S. President **Dwight D. Eisenhower** (*see*) denied American responsibility, but when faced with Powers's confession, he admitted that U-2 aircraft had been flying similar missions over the Soviet Union for four years. Soviet Premier **Nikita Khrushchev** (*see*) reacted strongly, expressing horror at what he called ''aggressive acts'' by the U.S. government. At the May 15 summit conference in Paris, originally called for by both nations to continue in the spirit of cooperation initiated in the Geneva summit of 1956, Khrushchev angrily demanded that Eisenhower apologize for the incident as a precondition to negotiations. When Eisenhower refused, Khrushchev withdrew an earlier invitation for a post-summit trip to Moscow. On August 16, Gary Powers was sentenced by a Soviet court to ten years "deprivation of freedom." In September, 1960, the U-2 incident generated further friction between the two nations during a meeting of the United Nations General Assembly in New York City when Khrushchev again spoke out against American spy flights over the Soviet Union. Emphasizing his outrage, the Soviet Premier removed his shoe and hammered it on the table.

U.S.S. NAUTILUS. The world's first nuclear-powered submarine, the *Nautilus* demonstrated the enormous potential of a submarine that could remain underwater for many weeks without surfacing or refueling. **Hyman Rickover** (*see*) envisioned the applicability of nuclear power to submarines as early as 1947, but it took almost a decade to win the support of the U.S. Navy for his *Nautilus* program and then to overcome the engineering problems of excess of heat and radioactivity generated by a nuclear reactor. Finally, in January, 1954, the *Nautilus*—323 feet long, carrying a crew of 105 at a cruise speed of twenty knots per hour—was successfully launched. Four years later, in August, 1958, a submerged voyage under the North Pole provided dramatic proof of the potential of nuclear submarines. Today's nuclear submarines can travel up to 400,000 miles on a single fuel charge.

W

WARREN, Earl (1891–1974). As the Chief Justice of the United States for 16 years (1953–1969), Warren presided over the Supreme Court during one of the most active periods in history. Born in Los Angeles, Warren resolved to become a lawyer after viewing criminal trials at the county courthouse as a high school teenager. In 1914, he was admitted to the California bar shortly after receiving a Doctor of Laws degree from the University of California at Berkeley. Warren served as a corporation lawyer before joining the Army from 1917–1918 as a training instructor. Warren rose through California's judicial ranks as Oakland city attorney (1919–1920), deputy to the district attorney of Alameda County (1920–1925), and district attorney (1925–1938). In 1938, he was elected attorney general of California after winning nomination by three parties—Republican, Democratic, and Progressive. Warren successfully combatted illegal gambling and racketeering, but he drew criticism for approving the internment of many Nisei (Japanese-Americans) during World War II. Warren was elected governor of California as a Republican in 1942, 1946, and 1950, becoming the state's only chief executive to serve three consecutive terms. As a largely nonpartisan governor, Warren instituted many social-welfare programs, reduced state sales taxes, and provided funds for state development. The keynote speaker at the Republican National Convention in 1944, Warren was nominated for President as California's "favorite son" candidate. In 1949, after contending for the nomination, Warren accepted **Thomas E. Dewey's** (*see*) invitation to run as the Republican Vice-Presidential candidate. However, the Dewey-Warren slate was defeated by a Democratic ticket headed by President **Harry S. Truman** (*see*). On September 30, 1953, President **Dwight D. Eisenhower** (*see*) appointed Warren Chief Justice of the Supreme Court to succeed the late Frederick M. Vinson (1890–1953). "I conceive of this Court," Warren said, "as the balance wheel of this government. Its function is to keep us from swinging too violently to one extreme or another." However, the Warren Court, as it was soon called by friends and critics alike, because one of the most liberal in the nation's history. On May 17, 1954, the Chief Justice wrote the landmark ruling in *Brown v. Board of Education of Topeka, Kansas* that initiated the federal government's efforts to desegregate the nation's public schools. Another important Warren Court ruling, *Miranda v. Arizona* (1965), established that citizens held in custody by the police must be informed of their right to an attorney and their right to refrain from incriminating themselves. Warren also wrote the opinion in *Powell v. McCormack* (1969), in which the Court decided that New York Representative **Adam Clayton Powell, Jr.** (*see*) had been illegally excluded from his seat in the House of Representatives in 1967. Retiring to private life on June 23, 1969, Warren was praised by President Richard M. Nixon (born 1913) for his integrity, fairness, and dignity. He was succeeded as Chief Justice by Warren E. Burger (born 1908).

UPI

Earl Warren (left) with the President after Warren E. Burger (right) was sworn in as new Chief Justice.